THE AUTHORITY ON™

WORKERS' COMPENSATION CLAIMS IN GEORGIA: THE DEFINITIVE GUIDE FOR INJURED VICTIMS & THEIR LAWYERS IN WORKERS' COMPENSATION CASES

BY:
GARY MARTIN HAYS

ISBN: 978-0-9962875-3-1

For more information, please write:
We Published That, L.L.C.
c/o Adam Weart
PO Box 956669
Duluth, GA 30095

DEDICATION

As you enter the building for my law firm, you will see a plaque hanging on the exterior wall to the right of the front door. It is a quote from the book of Proverbs in the Old Testament:

> *"Speak up for those who cannot speak up for themselves, for the rights of all who are destitute. Speak up and judge fairly; defend the rights of the poor and needy."*

When I walk into the building, it is a reminder to me and my staff of the tremendous opportunity we have to help people - often times through the most difficult times they have ever faced. I dedicate this book to all of those clients - 40,000 + and growing, who place their confidence and trust in me and my staff to help them with their cases.

This book is also dedicated to the attorneys and staff at the Law Offices of Gary Martin Hays & Associates, P.C. - not only for all of the hard work that they perform for our clients, but for the manner in which they do that work. They exemplify their care and compassion every time they pick up the phone or meet with a client at the firm. None of this would be possible without their assistance, and for that, I am eternally grateful.

I also want to dedicate this book to my wife, Sheri, and our daughters, Audrey, Ashleigh and Ava. God Bless ALL of you for the love and support you have given me!

Gary Martin Hays

Introduction

If you, a family member or friend has been injured on the job, then this book is for you. For over a quarter of a century, I have been an attorney in Georgia focusing on handling only workers' compensation, personal injury, and wrongful death claims. This book is a compilation of the laws in Georgia regarding workers' compensation claims condensed into an easy to read format. This is also a book filled with valuable nuggets of information from all of our years of experience helping over 40,000 clients since 1993.

When people are hurt on the job, they call our office with a lot of the same questions:

- Who will pay for my lost wages?

- How will I know if the workers' compensation checks I'm receiving are for the right amount?

- How long will the insurance company pay me workers' compensation checks?

- Who will pay for my medical bills?

- Do I have to treat with a company doctor?

- May I get an examination with a doctor I know and trust AND get the insurance company to pay for it?

- Who will pay for my prescriptions?

- The travel to the doctor and the physical therapist is expensive. Will I be reimbursed for my travel and parking?

- What benefits can I receive if my injuries are permanent?

- What happens if I can't work again?

- What are my rights?

- What are the employer and insurance company's responsibilities?

And there are many, many more questions!

These are certainly legitimate concerns and worries and you deserve answers. You need someone who is willing to fight to get you all the cash and benefits you are legally entitled to receive. Every single client needs an attorney that cares, that will take action, and will listen.

I suppose I learned best how to work with people when tragedy strikes from watching my father. For more than 50 years, he was a United Methodist Minister serving churches in south Alabama and northwest Florida. He was always there whenever someone needed to talk - never judging, but listening. It's funny how a lot of people just assume preachers only work on Saturdays for weddings and Sundays to preach - while mixing in the occasional funeral. His work never seemed to end. If the home phone wasn't ringing, there was a knock on the door from one of the members of the church or a friend of a friend who was a member that just wanted to talk.

Helping people who have been hurt at work or in a wreck is not a 9 to 5 type job nor commitment. It requires long hours, rolling up the sleeves, and a dedicated work ethic.

I am proud to say that we have helped over 40,000 victims and their families since 1993 in their car wreck, workers' compensation, wrongful death, inadequate security, and social security claims.

It has been an honor and a privilege to have helped these wonderful people through their trying times. I'm proud of what I do, and I'm thankful that the Good Lord has given me the opportunity to continue to work in this field.

It is my hope that this book will help guide injured victims and their attorneys through the mine fields that can exist in workers' compensation claims. Some attorneys would never let you peek behind the curtain to see how they handle cases. To me, there are no secrets. I want to share our knowledge with others so they can help Georgia's consumers take on the insurance industry. We want to educate our clients and others on their rights, as well as the employer's and insurance company's responsibilities.

Should you ever have any questions regarding the information contained in this book, please do not hesitate to contact me at Gary@GaryMartinHays.com. If you would like to have my law firm conduct a free, no obligation, completely confidential consultation of your workers' compensation claim, please do not hesitate to call. At a minimum, if you don't call us, please call someone - but please call someone who specializes in workers' compensation claims.

Our toll free phone number is 1 (888) 934-8100.
Or you can call (770) 934-8000.

One other note:

> The information we are sharing with you in this book is general in nature. It is not designed to provide specific legal advice regarding you and your potential claim. The information in this book may or may not apply to your specific case. Nothing can replace a consultation with an experienced attorney to discuss the facts about your particular claim.

> Further, should you have any desire to explore pursuing your potential claim, you should not delay as there are various statutes of limitation which could limit or completely bar your claims for recovery should you not pursue the matter in a timely fashion. We are NOT providing you information regarding the specific statute(s) of limitation applicable to your potential claim as this can only be determined after a detailed consultation of your case with an experienced attorney.

By providing you with this information, we are not giving you specific legal advice about your case, nor have we been retained to handle your claim unless you and our firm have entered into a written contract of representation regarding your potential legal claim.

I sincerely wish you all the best!

God Bless and Be Safe!

Gary Martin Hays

The Law Offices of
Gary Martin Hays & Associates, P.C.
3098 Breckinridge Boulevard
Duluth, GA 30096

(770) 934-8000
(888) 934-8100

www.GaryMartinHays.com

Table of Contents

CHAPTER 1 –
What is Workers' Compensation?

CHAPTER 1 – What is Workers' Compensation?

The workers' compensation system is perhaps the most misunderstood area of the law we have here in Georgia. Everyone seems to have an opinion about what you can and cannot do if you are injured on the job. We often hear:

- "I was told I could sue my employer in State Court."

- "I know a jury would award me a lot of money when they hear how I got hurt and about the unsafe working conditions at my job site."

- "People are getting hurt out there all the time. I know when the jury hears about all those other injuries, they will give me a big verdict."

- "I was told I could, either decide to get workers' comp benefits, or opt out and sue my employer."

- "My employer told me that if I filed for workers' comp benefits, the company would go bankrupt."

- "It doesn't matter if I had drugs in my system when I got hurt. I wasn't smoking marijuana when I was operating the saw."

- "I don't have to use the company doctor if I got hurt on the job."

- "My boss told me I can't recover workers' comp benefits because the car wreck was my fault."

Unfortunately, most of those "opinions" are completely wrong. To fully understand workers' compensation, it helps to have an understanding about why this system was created.

Before Georgia enacted the Workers' Compensation Act, **O.C.G.A. Section 34-9-1**, <u>et seq.</u>, the only way an injured worker could recover for injuries on the job against the employer was by filing a civil lawsuit. However, the employer could raise defenses to the lawsuit, including "assumption of the risk." This defense meant that the employee knew the work was dangerous, yet even knowing the risks, he continued to do the job. If he was hurt, he knew this was a possibility and therefore could not recover. It was an uphill battle for injured workers to recover benefits. A lot of injured workers would not pursue their claims; those that did often lost. For the few that did receive a verdict, it was extremely difficult to recover against the employer as the business was not insured and could not afford to pay the verdict. The employer would simply go out of business and the injured worker would still be left with medical bills, a disabling injury, and no safety net. This was not a good situation for the injured worker or the employer.

The Georgia legislature recognized that something had to be done to better protect the injured worker AND the employer. In 1920, our state passed the first workers' compensation laws. Over time, the system has evolved, but the basic tenets are still the same:

- The injured worker is able to recover:

- authorized medical expenses
- a percentage of lost wages and
- an additional sum if the injuries are permanent.

- The employer has to provide coverage if they have 3 or more employees.

- The employer has to cover the injured worker - regardless of fault - unless the injuries were caused by an intentional act of the employee, there was some willful misconduct on behalf of an employee that proximately caused the injury, or some deviation that prevented the accident from "arising out of and in the course and scope of the employment."

As a tradeoff:

- The employer is insulated from a civil lawsuit as he CANNOT be sued for pain and suffering, emotional suffering, or some other damages.

- The employer no longer has the risk or worry about having a large verdict rendered against the company for these damages.

- The "sole, exclusive remedy" for the injured worker is to file for workers' compensation benefits.

The Courts have made it very clear that the Workers' Compensation Act is to be "liberally construed" in favor of the injured worker or his/her dependents. Seckinger & Co. v. Foreman, 252 Ga. 540, 314 S.E.2d 891 (1984), citing General Motors Corp. v. Bowman, 107

Ga.App. 335, 338, 130 S.E.2d 163 (1963). In layman's terms, if it is 50/50 on whether or not the worker should get benefits, then the scale is always tipped in favor of the injured worker.

It is also important to keep in mind that you do not have to prove the employer was somehow negligent in causing your injuries for you to be eligible to receive workers' compensation benefits. In fact, you could be the one at fault in causing your injuries and it will not affect your eligibility. However, if you intentionally tried to hurt yourself, or you did not adhere to certain safety guidelines and procedures or use certain safety devices your employer had available for you, the injuries may not be covered.

One interesting thing to note about our workers' compensation system is that it is made up of laws passed by the legislature, as well as Rules passed by the State Board of Workers' Compensation. (See **O.C.G.A. Section 34-9-40**). Every state has its own system for handling workers' compensation claims. Procedures are different for filing claims, as are the potential benefits one may receive. The last thing you should do is compare your case to anyone else that is pursuing a workers' compensation claim - especially if their claim is governed by the laws of another state.

One must be experienced in navigating the laws and the Board Rules. If you or a family member or friend is injured on the job, I cannot stress to you enough the importance of hiring an attorney that has many years of experience handling workers' compensation claims. It is never a good idea to try and take on the insurance company and their team of lawyers by yourself either. It also is never smart to hire an attorney that is not a specialist in this area of the law. You have one chance at justice - one chance at maximizing your health and financial recovery. At a minimum, I encourage you to discuss your potential claim(s) with an attorney before you ever speak with the insurance company.

CHAPTER 2 –
Definitions: Employee and Employer

CHAPTER 2 – Definitions: Employee and Employer

> Did the Employer have the right or did the
> Employer assume the right to control the time,
> manner, methods and means of the work performed
> by the worker?[1]

The Court of Appeals has established a checklist of factors that can be used to determine whether or not an injured worker was an employee or an independent contractor:

(1) *How much control did the employer exercise over the details of the work?*

The more control the employer exercises over a worker, the more likely he/she will be considered an employee.[2] If the alleged employer has the right to "hire and fire" workers employed by a "subcontractor", then the courts will often find an employer/employee relationship.[3] However, if the "subcontractor" is the entity that has exclusive rights to "hire and fire" its workers, then the Georgia courts have held this supports the finding that the "subcontractor" is indeed an independent contractor.[4]

(2) *Is the worker engaged in a distant occupation or business?*

Is the worker doing the "regular" work of the business, or doing something that is separate and completely different?

---

[1] Echo Enterprises, Inc. v. Aspinwall, 194 Ga. App. 444, 390 S.E.2d 867 (1990); Burgett v. Thamer Construction, Inc., 165 Ga. App. 404, 300 S.E.2d 211 (1983); Simpkins v. Unigard Mutual Ins. Co., 130 Ga.App. 535, 203 S.E.2d 742 (1974).

[2] Employers Mutual Liability Ins. Co. V. Johnson, 104 Ga.App. 617, 122 S.E.2d 308 (1961).

[3] Clements v. Georgia Power Co., 148 Ga.App. 745, 252 S.E.2d 635 (1979).

[4] Simpkins v. Uniguard Mutual Ins. Co., 130 Ga.App. 535, 203 S.E.2d 742 (1974).

For example, a dentist's office may hire a cleaning company to send a worker to the dentist's office to clean it. The custodian would not be engaged in the occupation of being a dentist or a dental assistant, nor is his cleaning of the office in the dental "business." He is engaged in a distinct business of cleaning.

(3) ***Is the work performed normally done under supervision of the employer or by a specialist who does not need supervision?***

In other words, how much control does the "alleged employer" have over the worker? The greater the control exercised over the worker by the supervisor, the more likely the court will find an employer/employee relationship. [5]

(4) ***Is there skill or expertise required in performing the work?***

Does the subcontractor have a skill or expertise which the "alleged employer" does not have? The more skills and expertise the worker has and uses, which is outside the regular occupation or business of the "alleged employer", the more likely the court will find an independent contractor relationship.[6]

(5) ***Does the alleged employer provide tools and/or a place for the work to be performed?***

If the employer requires the worker to use the employer's

---

[5] R.E. Moss v. Central of Georgia Railroad Co., 135 Ga.App. 904, 219 S.E.2d 593 (1973).

[6] R.E. Moss v. Central of Georgia Railroad Co., 135 Ga.App. 904, 219 S.E.2d 593 (1973).

tools and materials for the job, this could be considered as a persuasive element leaning towards an employer/employee relationship.[7]

(6)   *Is there a set time for which the person is engaged in performing the contract?*

Also, does the Employer control the hours in which the work is to be performed? Is there a length of time in which the worker is employed that is set forth in the contract?

(7)   *How is the worker paid for the job?*

A worker that is paid by the hour or is paid a set salary leans more towards an employer/employee relationship. If the worker is paid based upon a set price for a finished job or specific amount of work, then it is more likely to be considered an independent contractor relationship.[8]

(8)   *Is the work that is being performed a part of the regular business of the alleged employer?*

This is very similar to factor (4) discussed previously.

A custodian cleaning a dentist's office is not performing work that is in the regular business of the alleged employer, especially if it is being done outside normal working hours. A dental hygienist that comes to work cleaning teeth would be performing work that is a regular part of the business of being a dentist.

(9)   *What was the intent of the parties? Did they*

---

[7] Simpkins v. Uniguard Mutual Ins. Co., 130 Ga.App. 535, 203 S.E.2d 742 (1974).
[8] Id.

*__intend to create an Employer/Employee
relationship, or that of an independent contractor?__*

This is one of the most important factors that a judge will
consider when deciding if there is an employer/employee
relationship. Was there a **written** contract of employment?
If so, were the terms clear that this was to be an
independent contractor relationship? Did it specify who
would be responsible for securing workers' compensation
insurance? Who was responsible for handling the taxes and
social security benefits for the worker? Were these
amounts withheld in the paychecks by the employer? If the
alleged worker is listed as "self-employed" on their tax
returns and was also responsible for paying their own taxes,
the more likely the relationship will be considered that of
an independent contractor.[9]

No one factor is completely determinative of your work
status; i.e., whether or not you are an employee or an
independent contractor. The Administrative Law Judge
will consider all of the factors and circumstances when
making their decision. I highly recommend you discuss the
specifics of your work situation with an experienced
attorney in the workers' compensation system to help you
decide whether or not you may be eligible for workers'
compensation benefits.

**How can you determine if your employer has workers'
compensation insurance**?

You can verify coverage by going to the State Board of

---

[9] R.E. Moss v. Central of Georgia Railroad Co., 135
Ga.App. 904, 219 S.E.2d 593 (1973). See also Simpkins
v. Uniguard Mutual Ins. Co., 130 Ga.App. 535, 203 S.E.2d
742 (1974).

Workers' Compensation website:
www.SBWC.Georgia.gov.

Click on the link entitled "How do I verify an employer's workers compensation insurance coverage?" You can search by employer in this section.

CHAPTER 3 –
What injuries are covered under Georgia's Workers' Compensation Act?

CHAPTER 3 – What injuries are covered under Georgia's Workers' Compensation Act?

Under Georgia law, the Workers' Compensation Act covers personal injuries, deaths, and occupational diseases that arise "out of and in the course of the employment . . ."[10]   If an employee is injured on the job while he is performing the duties that were assigned to him during his work hours, he is covered under Georgia's workers' compensation laws. The phrase "arising out of and in the course of employment" has been litigated since the beginning of the workers' compensation system's implementation here in Georgia, and there is no clear cut test. Here are some of the major points the court will consider in deciding whether or not the injury is compensable under workers' compensation:

- There must be a "causal connection" between the work and the injury.

- The injury must somehow relate to the job or be caused by the peculiar nature of the job.

- The accident and injury must somehow be because of the employment.

- It must occur within the time period of employment and at a place where the employee may reasonably be in the performance of their duties.

---

[10] **O.C.G.A. Section 34-9-1(4).**

Here are some examples of accidents and injuries where the courts ruled the accident and injury **did arise** out of and in the course and scope of the employment:

- Glens Falls Indemnity Co., et al., v. Sockwell[11]: a driver/salesman for a laundry service was driving his company's truck and taking a load of laundry from Atlanta to Carrollton. He was flagged down by some boys and girls whose car was broken down. At their request, he let them use a pair of pliers to work on their car. When that failed, he tried to help push their car with his truck but the bumpers became stuck. He got out of his truck and was successful in unlocking the bumpers. While heading back to his truck, he remarked "These boys are messing me up." He opened the door to the truck, put the pliers and flashlight in. He had one foot on the pavement, one foot on the running board of the truck, and his hand on the steering wheel - apparently in the act of re-entering his truck. All of a sudden, he was struck by a drunk driver traveling at a high rate of speed. He was knocked to the pavement and later died from his injuries. The Court of Appeals held his accident did arise out of the course and scope of his employment. Even if the actions he took to help the fellow travelers on the highway were considered a deviation to his employment, the

---

[11] 58 Ga. App. 111, 197 S.E. 647 (1938).

deviation ended when he was in the process of getting back into his truck to finish his delivery.

- Armour & Co. v. Little[12]: an employee had some fingers amputated while trying to remove particles of meat from a meat cutting machine. The employer argued that the employee's willful failure to use a certain rake - which was a safety device designed to be used for removing meat particles in the machine - caused his accident. Typically, willful misconduct, such as the failure to use a safety device, will bar a recovery under workers' compensation.

In this case, the employee demonstrated to the court that he never received any instruction on how or when to use the safety rake, and that his failure to use it was not willful but due to the lack of knowledge of the dangers. His claim was considered compensable and benefits were awarded.

- London Guarantee & Accident Co., et al. v. Herndon[13]: the employee was a soil cement engineer who traveled the southeast working with contractors and engineers on various projects for his employer. He had no set working hours, and would typically make out his reports of the day's activities after eating his evening meal. He was sent to Daytona Beach for a job by his employer, and his wife and daughter went with him to stay at an apartment while working at this location. He drove his

---

[12] 64 S.E.2d 707, 83 Ga.App. 762 (1951).
[13] 81 Ga. App. 178, 58 S.E.2d 510 (1950).

wife and child to Daytona in his company car to get some food because the apartment where they were staying was not equipped for them to fix meals. While returning back to their apartment after dinner so he could complete his reports, he decided to take a road that ran along the beach. He thought he was taking an access that would allow him to return to the highway. However, his car became stuck in the sand. He asked his wife and daughter to try and find some lumber or other debris they could put under the wheels to help the wheels of the car gain traction. When his family returned back to the car, they found the car had fallen and trapped him under it, causing his death. The court ruled that the employee was on his way back to his apartment to complete his work for the employer. The fact that he deviated for personal reasons down the beach route does not in an of itself negate the claim for benefits. The court opined that traveling salesman typically do not have a regular schedule of working hours and that "[A]ctivities, the performance of which are necessary to his health and comfort, while in a sense personal to himself, are nevertheless incidents of his employment and acts of service within the meaning of the Workmen's Compensation Act."[14] When the employee attempted to turn back to make out his daily reports, he resumed the duties of his employment and therefore his death was ruled as compensable and his surviving family members were able to recover death benefits under workers' compensation.

---

[14] Id. at 512.

- W.L. Pike v. Maryland Casualty Company, et al.[15]: the deceased employee was a district office and sales manager for his employer, and he had duties which included selling houses, as well as the authority to hire other salesman. According to the company's representative at the hearing, there was no such thing as being "off duty", as they worked late into the evenings, and had considerable latitude in their dealings to get a job done. One night, the deceased employee set up a meeting with a gentleman at a night club to see if he could help him round up business prospects in the Fort Stewart area. He would pay this man a commission on each house he was able to sell to these leads. After meeting with this man again at a night club, the worker was killed in a car furnished to him by the employer while returning home. The Court of Appeals concluded that "[S]elling includes finding prospects."[16] Meeting with the man to see if he could help generate leads and prospects was reasonably necessary and incidental to his work, and therefore, arose out of and in the course and scope of his employment. Death benefits were awarded to his surviving spouse.

- General Fire & Casualty Co., et al., v. Bellflower, et al.[17]: the deceased employee

---

[15]

[16] Id. at 80.

Bellflower was a bus driver from Macon who was killed while "off duty" between trips in Jacksonville, Florida. After his route ended, the employer provided a hotel room at the Floridian that was near the bus station for rest and sleeping. If he stayed at another hotel, the expenses incurred were not necessarily reimbursable. That night, another employee telephoned Bellflower and asked him to go get something to eat near the hotel. While returning to the hotel after the meal, the two were accosted by a criminal assailant who shot and killed Bellflower. The Court of Appeals held that the shooting was not a willful act by the assailant directed against Bellflower for reasons personal to the employee. The court equated the bus driver to the status of a traveling salesman who has to be away from home for the night, writing "[S]uch an employee is in continuous employment, day and night."[18] He was required to eat, and was returning back to his hotel to get the rest that was required to be able to drive the bus when he was shot. When the assault on Bellflower was found not to be for personal reasons, the fact that he was walking back from a meal in a high crime area on account of his employment was enough to show that the death arose out of his employment. Death benefits were awarded to his survivors.

- Harris v. Peach County Board of Commissioners[19]: Harris worked as a custodian

---

[17] 123 Ga. App. 864, 182 S.E.2d 678 (1971).
[18] Id. at 681.
[19] 296 Ga. App. 225, 674 S.E.2d 36 (2009).

in the Peach County Courthouse. While out on the floor with her cleaning cart, she went to get some paper towels and tissues to restock the restrooms. When she was walking back to the restroom, she stopped in the hall to discuss work issues with her supervisor. During this conversation, Harris notice that a diuretic pill that she previously put in her pocket was no longer there. Her supervisor saw it on the floor, and pointed it out to Harris. When she bent over to pick it up, she "heard something pop in her left knee and collapsed."[20] She was diagnosed with an anterior dislocation of her left knee that required her to undergo two surgeries. As a result of this, she applied for disability benefits. The Court of Appeals reviewed the evidence that was presented at her hearing. Harris's job duties required her to pick up foreign objects on the floor, even if it was her own pill. The court also learned that Harris was over-weight, weighing slightly just under 300 pounds. The weight may have made her more susceptible to sustaining the knee injury, and could have happened at any time. However, "[I]t is well established that an employee need not be in perfect health or free from disease at the time received the injury under the Act; the employer takes his employee as it finds him and assumes the risk of a diseased condition aggravated by injury."[21] The Court found that picking up the medicine off of the floor - even though it was hers and she planned on taking it instead of throwing it away - was still in the

---

[20] Id. at 226.
[21] Id. at 229.

course and scope of her employment so benefits
were awarded.

These are some cases where the courts have ruled the
accidents and injuries **did not** arise out of and in the course
and scope of employment:

- Davis v. Houston General Ins. Co.[22]: a nurse's aide
  was reaching back to put her left arm into her coat
  sleeve as she was getting ready to leave work at the
  end of her shift. She felt a "pop" in her left arm.
  The Court of Appeals held that there was absolutely
  no evidence to show that the "pop" which occurred
  was in any way related to or caused by the peculiar
  nature of her job duties. Therefore, her claim for
  worker's compensation benefits was denied.

- Borden Foods Company v. Dorsey[23]: an employee
  of Borden Foods was "walking along an aisle
  marked off on the concrete floor of the employer's
  plant and proceeding to her place of work in another
  part of the plant . . ."[24] An eyewitness testified that
  it appeared the employee might have fainted or had
  a muscle give out when she fell to the floor. The
  employee did not strike any equipment or anything
  other than the floor when she fell.
  The court ruled that the claim was not compensable
  as "the claimant's fall resulted from an idiopathic
  condition, and that the injury she sustained as a
  result thereof was no greater than it would have

---

[22] 141 Ga. App. 385, 233 S.E.2d 479 (1977).
[23] 112 Ga. App. 838, 146 S.E.2d 532 (1965).
[24] Id. at 534.

been had she suffered a similar fall on a hard surface at any place other than on the employer's premises."[25]

- Prudential Bank, et al., v. Moore[26]: the employee worked as a computer clerk for Prudential. When she was confronted by her supervisors about numerous errors in her work, she blamed them on problems she was having with her vision. Shortly after this, she fell at work, apparently from a fainting episode, and struck her head on the baseboard. She complained of injuries such as diplopia (double vision), headaches, neck pain, and carpal tunnel syndrome. The Court of Appeals held that idiopathic falls - falls that occur for some unknown reason - are not typically covered under workers' compensation unless the employee "strikes some object specifically related to the work place, such as a work bench, machinery or equipment, because of the 'increased risk' cause by the presence of the work related object."[27] The court denied her claim as being compensable writing that "[A] wall and baseboard is not peculiar to the employment and thus does not fit the exception to non-coverage."[28]

UNEXPLAINED DEATHS:

What happens when an employee is found dead at work, or in a place where one would reasonably expect him to be at work? Over the years, the court has come up with what has

---

[25] Id.
[26] 219 Ga. App. 847, 467 S.E.2d 7 (1996).
[27] Id. at 8.
[28] Id.

been called a "natural presumption" that the death arose out of and in the course and scope of the employee's employment.

According to <u>Odom v. Transamerica Ins. Group</u>[29], when a worker is found at a place where one might reasonably expect that worker to be in the performance of his/her job duties, then there is a presumption that it arose out of and in the course and scope of the employment. If the employer and insurance company can show by affirmative evidence that the death **did not** arise out of the employment, then they can rebut the presumption.[30]

The courts apparently do not apply this presumption that the death arose out of and in the course and scope of employment to heart attack cases. In <u>G & H Logging, Inc., et al., v. Burch</u>[31], the deceased employee, Willie Lee Burch, was a truck driver for a logging company. On September 1, 1982, he drove his truck cab to a site in the woods that morning. He threw chains over some logs that were previously loaded onto a trailer, tightened the chains, and then began driving the tractor trailer out of the woods towards the highway. Another employee who also drove a log truck followed the same route that Mr. Burch took a little over an hour later. As he approached the gate leading to the highway, he noticed Mr. Burch's tractor and fully loaded trailer on the side of the road before the gate as though it was deliberately parked there. He kept going to make his delivery. On his return trip, he saw the rig still parked in the same location. He got out to investigate and

---

[29] 148 Ga. App. 156, 251 S.E.2d 48 (1978).

[30] <u>Southern Bell Tel. and Tel. Co. v. Hodges</u>, 164 Ga. App. 757, 298 S.E.2d 570 (1982).

[31] 178 Ga. App. 28, 341 S.E.2d 868 (1986).

discovered Mr. Burch lying dead on the floor of the truck's cab. The coroner concluded on the death certificate that the immediate cause of the death was "coronary occlusion."[32] The Court of Appeals ruled that the case was controlled by Brown Transp. Corp. v. Blanchard[33], citing **O.C.G.A. Section 34-9-1(4)**. This section provides that " . . . nor shall 'injury' and 'personal injury' include heart disease, heart attack, the failure or occlusion of any of the coronary blood vessels, or thrombosis, unless it is shown by a preponderance of competent and credible evidence that it was attributable to the performance of the usual work of employment."[34] The court reviewed the evidence at the initial hearing on the claim. "The [deceased was not required to perform any strenuous work or activity as part of his job on September 1, 1982. The logs he transported were already loaded onto the trailer and he had only to put the chains securing the load over the logs and tighten these down. The truck he drove was air conditioned, had power steering, and other convenience."[35] Mr. Burch was also a very heavy smoker, observed to be sickly, and often at a loss of breath. In light of these factors, the Court of Appeals opined that there was ample evidence to conclude his death was from a heart attack and the work he did on the date of his death was not a precipitating or aggravating cause.[36] Therefore, death benefits were denied.

---

[32] Id. at 868.
[33] 126 Ga. App. 333, 190 S.E.2d 625 (1972).
[34] Id. at 870.
[35] Id. at 869.
[36] Id. at 870.

<u>Horseplay</u>:

If a worker or workers start engaging in horseplay or practical jokes, the courts generally rule that these accidents and injuries do not arise out of and in the course and scope of the employment. In <u>A.J. Kight v. Liberty Mutual Insurance et al.</u>[37], the injured worker and other employees engaged in a fair amount of horseplay around the office. Two employees in particular had a little battle going on which involved one (Mr. Fussell) getting hit on the nose with a clipboard on one day by Mr. Kight, and the next morning getting his face jabbed with a fist - also by Mr. Kight. After these two incidents, Mr. Fussell pulled a chair out from under Mr. Kight, resulting in his injury. Mr. Kight filed for workers' compensation benefits and the application was denied by the Administrative Law Judge, next by the Full Board, and then the Superior Court. The Court of Appeals affirmed the denial of benefits to Mr. Kight as well, writing "[A]ny accident and injury suffered by the claimant, Allen J. Kight, was caused by the wilful act of a third person directed against the claimant for personal reasons. The accident and the injury to the claimant, although occurring in the course of his employment, did not arise out of the claimant's employment." **Id.**, at 454. However, it should be noted that the Court has held that if the injured worker was not a participant in the horseplay, but was merely an innocent bystander performing their work in the course and scope of their employment, then their claim would be considered compensable and covered by the Workers' Compensation Act of Georgia.[38]

---

[37] 141 Ga. App. 409, 233 S.E.2d 453 (1977).

Ingress and Egress

There has been a lot of litigation over whether or not injuries that occur in the parking lot or on the premises of the employer are considered covered under workers' compensation. As a general rule, when employees are coming into work or are leaving work on the grounds of the employer, the premises are considered a part of the employer's business which provides enough of the "work" connection to render the case covered under workers' compensation.[39] To be compensable, the accident does not necessarily have to occur after the employee is clocked in and ready to work. The law allows a reasonable time for ingress and egress while on the employer's premises.[40]

To and From Work

Accidents that happen while an employee is driving to and from work are generally not covered under the Workers' Compensation Act of Georgia. In Mark The Mover v. Lancaster[41], Roland Lancaster was employed at the moving company as an office worker. The company was owned and operated by his son-in-law, Richard Whitehead. Mr. Lancaster's job duties involved "answering the telephone, making moving arrangements, repairing furniture, and occasionally moving furniture."[42] If the company needed

---

[38] American Mutual Liability Ins. Co., et al., v. Benford, 77 Ga. App. 93, 47 S.E.2d 673 (1948).

[39] U.S. Cas. Co. V. Russell, 98 Ga. App. 181, 105 S.E.2d 378. (1958).

[40] Id. at 378. See also DeHowitt v. Hartford Fire Ins. Co., 99 Ga. App. 147, 108 S.E.2d 280 (1959).

[41] 234 Ga. App. 319, 506 S.E.2d 673 (1998).

[42] Id. at 319.

him to make deliveries, he would either use the company truck or drive his own van. They also provided him with a pager so they could reach him as needed. When his car broke down in December 1995, Lancaster started walking to work every day. When he got tired of walking to and from work, he borrowed Mr. Whitehead's personal vehicle on January 18, 1996, until he could get his van repaired. Mr. Whitehead did not put any restrictions on how the vehicle could be used. The next morning, Lancaster stopped for breakfast on his way in to work. Several times during breakfast, he was paged by employer. When he tried to call in to the office, the line was always busy so he left the restaurant to head into work. As luck would have it, while on his way to work he was involved in a car accident.

Mr. Lancaster did admit at the hearing that he would have driven to work after breakfast even if he never received the pages.

The Administrative Law Judge and the Full Board denied the claim for benefits. The Superior Court, however, reversed the decision. The Court of Appeals reversed the Superior Court and denied the claim for benefits. Citing Corbin v. Liberty Mut. Ins. Co.,[43] the court wrote that "[G]enerally, injuries sustained on the way to and from work are not compensable."

The Court did note some exceptions:

    (1)   Where the employer furnishes transportation to the employee for the mutual benefit of the employee and the employer in order to further the employee's work, the claim may be compensable; and

---

[43] 117 Ga. App. 823, 162 S.E.2d 226 (1968).

> (2)　Where the employee must be available to the employer and is "on call" and the employer provides transportation costs or reimburses these costs, an injury to or from work may be compensable.[44]

In this case, the Court found that neither exception applied to Mr. Lancaster. Mark The Mover did furnish the transportation as an incident to his employment and for the mutual benefit of both to facilitate his work. The son-in-law was merely doing his father-in-law a favor by providing his the transportation.

Also, even though Mr. Lancaster had the pager and may have been "on call", the court noted that status stopped when he didn't have his car and started using his son-in-law's. The Court noted he would have been driving to work anyway - even if he did not receive the page - when the wreck happened.[45]

Mixed Purpose Trips

If an employee is required to travel in their employment, there is usually enough of a connection to work that the claim will be considered to "arise out of and in the course and scope of employment" and make the claim compensable.[46]   Questions about the compensability of the claim arise when there is a deviation from the employment by the employee for purely personal reasons. If an accident happens when the employee is on a personal deviation, then this is generally held to be a non-compensable accident.

---

[44] Id. at 320.

[45] Id.

[46] Boyd Bros. Transp. Co., Inc., v. Fonville, 237 Ga. App. 721, 516 S.E.2d 573 (1999).

However, once the employee is through with the detour or personal deviation and has resumed the duties of the employer, then the claim is typically considered compensable.

In United States Fid. & Guar. Co. v. Skinner,[47] the employer requested that the employee come to the company office in Savannah from the employee's home in Macon. The trip was at the expense of the employer and in a car furnished to the employee by the employer. The employee went to Savannah and checked in at a hotel. However, before he reported to the employer, he decided to drive an additional 18 miles to Tybee Island so he could "get a seafood dinner and see the ocean."[48] This was obviously a personal trip and there was no benefit to the employer. While driving the company car to Tybee, a tire blew out causing the vehicle to overturn seriously injuring the employee. He died three days later. The Supreme Court of Georgia finally heard the case and ruled that the employee's deviation was personal and did not arise out of nor in the course and scope of his employment. The Court wrote "[T]he salesmen had come to Savannah on a special call for a conference with the vice president of the company. It was not essential nor reasonably necessary to that conference nor in furtherance of the company's business that they should eat a sea-food dinner, and see the ocean."[49] Therefore, the claim for compensation benefits to the surviving family was denied.

The Georgia Court of Appeals found the employee's car wreck arose out of and in the course and scope of their employment in the case of Lewis v. Chatham County

---

[47] 188 Ga. 823, 5 S.E.2d 9 (1939).

[48] Id. at 10.

[49] Id. at 14.

Savannah Metropolitan Planning Commission, et al.[50]

In this claim, Lewis had her employer's permission to use the employer's car for "doing personal banking, running an errand for the employer, and performing banking activities for the employer."[51]

On the date of her accident, Lewis left the office to handle her employer's banking needs. Before doing that, she deviated from that route to have lunch in another part of the city. When she realized she was not going to have enough time for lunch, she turned around towards the bank to handle her employer's banking. While heading towards the bank, the collision occurred.

The Administrative Law Judge and the Full Board found the employee's deviation slight, and awarded Lewis benefits. The Superior Court reversed as it concluded the deviation "was significant, that Lewis had no permission to be where she was at the time of the collision, and that even though Lewis had turned back, she was still deviating from her permitted use of the employer's vehicle at the time of the collision."[52] The Court of Appeals adopted the findings of the Full Board, as the court felt her deviation was slight and she had resumed her employer's business before the wreck occurred.[53]

Fights On The Job

How does the Workers' Compensation Act view fights on the job? Are they covered? The Court of Appeals answered this in the case of City of Atlanta v. Shaw.[54] The

---

[50] 217 Ga. App. 534, 458 S.E.2d 173 (1995).
[51] Id.
[52] Id.
[53] Id. at 534-535.

employee, Shaw, worked as a water plant operator for the City of Atlanta.

She filed a claim for workers' compensation benefits after she was injured during a fight with a co-worker. The Court of Appeals wrote that "the record reveals no evidence that the dispute between the appellee and her co-worker was anything other than a personal one. Although the evidence is conflicting as to whether it was appellee or her co-worker who initiated the physical fight, it is uncontroverted that the verbal disagreement between the two which led to the fight concerned their use of appellant's telephone for their respective personal calls. It is also uncontroverted that there was a history of personal animosity between appellee and her co-worker."[55] The Court held that the employee was not doing any of the tasks that were required of her by her employer when she fought her co-worker and sustained her injuries. Therefore, her injuries did not arise out of and in the course and scope of her employment so benefit were denied.

Personal Breaks

If an employee is on a **scheduled break** and his/her employer does not exercise any control over the worker, an accident which results to an injury to the employee will not be covered by workers' compensation. This ruling was set forth in the case of Wilkie v. Travelers Ins. Co.[56]
In Wilkie, the employee was injured when she fell while on her way to the restroom during a ten-minute **scheduled** rest break.

---

[54] 179 Ga. App. 148, 345 S.E.2d 642 (1986).
[55] Id. at 643.
[56] 124 Ga. App. 714, 185 S.E.2d 783 (1971).

As the Court of Appeals wrote, "in 'lunch break' and 'rest break' cases, both the Supreme Court and this court have laid down the rule that where the employee is free to use the time as he chooses so that it is personal to him, an injury occurring during this time arises out of his individual pursuit and not out of his employment."[57]

In the case of Edwards v. Liberty Mutual Insurance Company, et al.[58], Lurene Edwards worked as a seamstress in a garment factory. She was injured when she went to the bathroom, not during a scheduled rest break, but at an unscheduled time after the morning break. She filed a claim for workers' compensation benefits. At the trial level, the judge found that Ms. Edwards did sustain an injury which should be covered under workers' compensation. The Full Board affirmed, but the superior court reversed the finding and the case was appealed to the Court of Appeals. The court ruled that it was well settled that if an employer provides employees with scheduled rest breaks where they are free to use the time as they choose, then if the worker is hurt during this time, the injury will not be covered under workers' compensation. The court refused to extend the rule to situations regarding unscheduled work breaks, however. "[w]hen the employee finds it necessary to go to the rest room, even though he is permitted to do so without obtaining permission from his supervisor", it is not the employee's free time as it cannot be considered an "altogether personal pursuit, as is the case during scheduled breaks."[59] Therefore, Ms. Edwards was

---

[57] Id. at 714.
[58] 130 Ga. App. 23, 202 S.E.2d 208 (1973)
[59] Id. at 210-211.

successful in recovering her workers' compensation benefits.

Acts of God

In <u>McKiney v. Reynolds & Manley Lumber Co.</u>[60], Mr. McKiney was a common laborer that worked in the employer's lumber yard as a "lumber stacker." This job required him to stack lumber and load the lumber onto vehicles. He and another co-employee loaded a wagon full of lumber. The other worker went to get a tractor driver to come and get the load. Mr. McKiney waited next to the lumber pile, and was leaning against it when, "without warning a bolt of lightning struck the deceased, causing instant death."[61] A claim was filed for workers' compensation benefits by his widow. The Administrative Law Judge denied benefits, finding "as a matter of fact that the deceased did not sustain an accidental injury which arose out of an in the course and scope of employment."[62] The claimant's widow appealed the ruling to the Superior Court of Chatham County and the judge affirmed the prior ruling denying compensation.

The Court of Appeals reversed the denial of benefits and awarded death benefits to the widow. "The evidence shows that the employee was where his duties required him to be, in the large lumber yard among stacks of wet or damp lumber, and the finding was demanded that by reason of his employment he was exposed to a hazard not equally shared by the community.

---

[60] 79 Ga. App. 826, 54 S.E.2d 471 (1949).
[61] <u>Id.</u> at 472.
[62] <u>Id.</u> at 471.

The test is not whether the injury was caused by an act of God, but whether the one injured was by his employment specially endangered by the act of God, be it lightning, tornado or windstorm."[63] (Citing Maryland Casualty Company v. Lilly, 62 Ga.App. 806, 10 S.E. 2d 110.

Intoxication

According to **O.C.G.A. Section 34-9-17(b)**,

> "No compensation shall be allowed for an injury or death due to intoxication by alcohol or being under the influence of marijuana or a controlled substance, except as may have been lawfully prescribed by a physician for such employee and taken in accordance with such prescription:"

In **O.C.G.A. Section 34-9-17(b)(1)**, the statute sets forth the specifics of "intoxication" more fully:

> "If the amount of alcohol in the employee's blood within three hours of the time of the alleged accident, as shown by chemical analyses of the employee's blood, urine, breath, or other bodily substance, is 0.08 grams or greater, there shall be a rebuttable presumption that the accident and injury or death were caused by the consumption of alcohol;"

In Communications, Inc., et al. v. Cannon et al.[64], Fred

---

[63] Id. at 473.
[64] 174 Ga.App. 820, 331 S.E.2d 112 (1985).

Cannon, Jr., was working for his employer as a construction superintendent. On December 22, 1982, Cannon was commuting home to Macon, Georgia driving a company truck from his place of employment in Valdosta, Georgia, where he had attended a company barbecue dinner.

He was killed in a head-on collision on the interstate after traveling approximately 1.5 miles southbound in the northbound lane. When Cannon's blood alcohol level was tested, it showed a level of .23 grams at his death.

The Administrative Law Judge denied the claim for death benefits filed by his widow. The Full Board affirmed the denial of benefits. When appealed, the Superior Court of Houston County reversed and benefits were awarded. The Court of Appeals held "[T]he full board was authorized to find Cannon's wilful misconduct in driving with a blood-alcohol level of .23 percent, proceeding the wrong way onto an exit ramp marked with signs indicating that he was going the wrong way, and then driving southbound for approximately 11.5 miles in the northbound lane of an interstate highway. Such conduct resulted in the head-on collision which killed Cannon. The full board was, thus, warranted in concluding that Cannon's death was not compensable under **O.C.G.A. Section 34-9-17**."[65]

Please note that the mere presence of alcohol or marijuana in the system is not enough to completely bar the claim if the injured worker can show that the injury was not caused because of the intoxicating alcohol or drug. In Lastinger v. Mill & Machinery, Inc. et al.[66], James Lastinger, Jr., worked as a steelworker with Mill & Machinery, Inc.

---

[65] Id. at 114.

[66] 236 Ga.App. 430, 512 S.E.2d 327 (1999).

He was hurt at work when a metal plate he was detaching from a conveyor belt broke loose, causing him to fall several feet to the floor below. He was taken to the emergency room and a urine sample tested positive for cocaine and marijuana.

Lastinger filed an application for workers' compensation benefits, but the employer/insurer controverted his claim based upon the positive drug test. Lastinger admitted at the hearing that he had used drugs five days before his injury but he denied being impaired on the day of his injury. Testimony was also presented at the hearing by a co-worker as well as his supervisor that Lastinger "did not appear to be intoxicated or unsteady."[67] Evidence was also introduced at the hearing of Lastinger's prior drug conviction for marijuana possession.

The Administrative Law Judge denied the claim for benefits "because Lastinger's own testimony was impeached by the copy of the certified misdemeanor conviction for marijuana possession, which the ALJ considered a crime of moral turpitude."[68] The Full Board and the Superior Court affirmed the denial of benefits, and the case was appealed. The Court of Appeals reversed, as it found the "sole basis for the appellate division's finding that Lastinger's testimony had been impeached was the misdemeanor conviction."[69] The Court felt the misdemeanor conviction never should have been introduced into evidence as a misdemeanor conviction for

---

[67] Id. at 431.
[68] Id.
[69] Id.

marijuana possession is not a crime of moral turpitude and should not have been allowed to impeach Lastinger.

The Court of Appeals remanded the case to the State Board of Workers' Compensation to determine "whether Lastinger's testimony was otherwise impeached without using the misdemeanor marijuana conviction and whether the presumption arising under **O.C.G.A. Section 34-9-17(b)** was rebutted."[70]

Cumulative Trauma

What happens if an "injury" occurs over time - and it is difficult for the injured worker to determine a specific date of injury? In <u>D.W. Adcock, M.D., P.C. et al. v. Adcock</u>[71], Dr. Adcock worked for a professional corporation that employed him as an orthopedic surgeon. After 25 years of work as a surgeon, he developed a disabling skin condition known as severe eczema or contact dermatitis that prevented him from continuing his profession as a surgeon. At the hearing, expert evidence was tendered that demonstrated the condition "was caused and aggravated by the intense scrubbing that was required prior to each surgery and by the in-office cleansing (averaging 50 times per day) required before seeing each patient. Adcock could point to no specific instance causing the onset of the condition."[72] It reached a point where Adcock was forced to stop working as a surgeon. Adcock filed a claim for workers' compensation benefits. The ALJ awarded benefits, and the Full Board affirmed. The Employer/Insurer argued to the Court of Appeals that Dr. Adcock's condition was a disease, not an injury, and

---

[70] <u>Id</u>.
[71] 257 Ga. App. 700, 572 S.E.2d 45 (2003)
[72] <u>Id</u>.

therefore it was not compensable. The Court held that "[C]umulative trauma over time, which does not lend itself to identifying a specific incident or date as the onset of the injury, nevertheless may be found to be an injury under this statute. See <u>Shipman v. Employers Mut. Liability Ins. Co.</u>, 105 Ga. App. 487, 488-493, 125 S.E.2d 72 (1962)."[73]

Aggravation or Acceleration of a Pre-Existing Condition

Georgia law recognizes the fact that employees may have a pre-existing problem when they step foot on their employer's work site. According to <u>Lumbermens Mut. Cas. Co. V. Griggs</u>, "Fortunately for the employee, perfect health is not a prerequisite to the enjoyment of benefits of this statute."[74] This means the employer cannot argue that the employee would not have been hurt had he/she been completely healthy. [75] However, there are limitations as the employer is only liable "for so long as the aggravation of the pre-existing condition continues to be the cause of the disability; the pre-existing condition shall no longer meet this criteria when the aggravation ceases to be the cause of the disability."[76]

Here are a couple of cases where the courts have held that a pre-existing condition was aggravated and the claim was compensable:

- Employee had a non-work related, pre-existing ruptured disk that required her to be hospitalized for

---

[73] <u>Id</u>. at 702.

[74] 190 Ga. 277, 288, 9 S.E.2d 84 (1940).

[75] See <u>Davis v. Bibb Mfg. Co.</u>, 75 Ga. App. 515, 43 S.E.2d 780 (1947).

[76] This is codified at O.C.G.A. Section 34-9-1(4).

a period of time. She was subsequently able to return to work and perform her assigned duties. When she returned to work she was pain free. However, she sustained an injury "while putting up a stock of hosiery she overturned a carton, went down on her knee, and felt her back 'pop', experienced immediate pain and again had to be hospitalized" and she was totally disabled as a result.[77] The Court of Appeals held that was an accepted accident and injury as it was the aggravation of a pre-existing condition.

- Employee was born with a condition known as spinal spondylolisthesis. The condition caused "back weakness because of a defect in the pedicle of the fifth lumbar vertebra so that it and the adjoining vertebra were not properly joined together by a bone connection."[78] The Employee was not having any problems with his back until he started working as a welder for Ford, a job that required "stooping, lifting and bending for long periods of time in awkward positions."[79] After five months of work, his back pain became disabling. He quit work and sought medical treatment for his condition. At a hearing requested by the Employee for benefits, the ALJ denied benefits as there was no injury, finding "Claimant was engaged in a job which he was not physically able to perform, showed no damage to his back caused by his job, and the only symptom which he has shown is that of

---

[77] S.S. Kresge Company v. Bryant, 123 Ga. App. 412, 181 S.E.2d 312 (1971).

[78] Thomas v. Ford Motor Co., 123 Ga.App. 512, 181 S.E.2d 874 (1971), at 875.

[79] Id.

pain which resulted from performing work which he was not physically equipped to perform due to a pre-existing congenital deformity." [80] The Court of Appeals reversed and stressed two points:

(1)   The aggravation of a pre-existing infirmity, whether congenital or otherwise, is compensable.[81]

(2)   Where a disability results that is objectively, physiologically ascertainable, "it is compensable although the onset of disability is imperceptible from day to day, and there is no one 'accident' at a specifiable time and place to which the result may be attributable"[82], citing Shipman v. Employers Mut. Liab. Ins. Co., 105 Ga. App. 487, 125 S.E.2d 72.

---

[80] Id.

[81] Id. at 876.

[82] Id.

CHAPTER 4 – Benefits to injured workers:
Indemnity, Medical, Permanent Partial Disability

CHAPTER 4 – Benefits to injured workers: Indemnity, Medical, Permanent Partial Disability

Under Georgia's Workers' Compensation system, there are three (3) types of benefits an injured worker may be eligible to receive. These are:

(1)   Indemnity Benefits (wage benefits);
(2)   Medical Benefits; and
(3)   Permanent Partial Disability Benefits (PPD).

Too many times, people assume that you are also able to receive money for pain and suffering and emotional suffering - benefits to compensate an injured worker for all the hassles they have endured and will endure because of their on the job injury. Unfortunately, the law limits the benefits to the three listed above. An injured worker is prohibited from filing a lawsuit and having their case by a jury. If there is any dispute as to whether or not an injured worker is entitled to receive any of the benefits listed above, the issue is heard and decided by an Administrative Law Judge - not by a jury.

One other thing to note about Georgia' Workers' Compensation system. It is designed to discourage injured workers from filing claims for minor accidents. It is also set up to encourage injured workers to return to work as quickly as possible. The way this is accomplished is by limiting the types of benefits an injured worker can receive, as well as the amount - in some instances - the injured worker can recover.

The three types of benefits are more fully discussed below:

(1)   **Indemnity Benefits**:

Indemnity benefits are checks that are paid to an injured worker to replace an employee's wages during their period of work-related disability. According to **O.C.G.A. Section 34-9-220**, no wage benefits are due to an injured worker unless they have been disabled by the authorized treating physician for seven calendar days. Benefits will vest beginning with the eight (8th) day of disability. If the injured worker is disabled for 21 consecutive days, then the employer insurer must pay the employee for the first seven calendar days of disability.[83] The employer does have the option, though not an obligation, to continue paying the employee regular wages during the disability period. If this is done, no workers' compensation indemnity benefits are due.[84]

The amount of indemnity benefits due to an injured worker is calculated according to a formula set forth under **O.C.G.A. Section 34-9-260**. The goal of the formula is to calculate the worker's average weekly wage. Once one determines the employee's average weekly wage, you can then calculate the amount of the indemnity benefits due the injured worker.

The usual method for calculating the average weekly wage is as follows:

(1)   Add the wages earned by the employee

---

[83] **O.C.G.A. Section 34-9-220**.
[84] See **Board Rule 220(c)**.

during the 13 weeks immediately preceding the on the job injury;

(2)   Divide this total by 13;

(3)   This amount is the average weekly wage.[85]

What happens if the injured worker did not work a substantial part of the 13 week period immediately preceding the on the job injury? The law instructs the employer/insurer to calculate the average weekly wage using the wages of a "similarly situated employee" that has worked the 13 week period.[86] If neither method can fairly or reasonably be applied to calculate the average weekly wage for the employee, then the "full-time weekly wage of the injured employee shall be used."[87]

It is interesting to note that Board Rule 260(a) provides a more expansive list of items that may be included in calculating the average weekly wage:

> "Computation of wages shall include, in addition to salary, hourly pay, or tips, the reasonable value of food, housing, and other benefits furnished by the employer without charge to the employee which constitute a financial benefit to the employee and are capable of pecuniary calculation."[88]

However, the Court of Appeals has ruled that the term "average weekly wage"**does not** include fringe benefits under **O.C.G.A. Section 34-9-260** though Board Rule 260

---

[85] **O.C.G.A. Section 34-9-260**.

[86] Id.

[87] Id.

[88] Board Rule 260(a).

authorizes this. If there is a conflict between the statutes and the board rules, the statute trumps the Board Rule.[89] In the case of <u>Groover v. Johnson Controls World Service</u>[90], Groover was injured and was disabled for a long enough period of time that the employer/insurer was required to commence indemnity benefits. The employer/insurer took the wages for the 13 weeks immediately preceding his on the job injury and calculated his average weekly wage. The employer/insurer did not take into account a shoe allowance the employee received, nor did they factor in the value of the employer's contributions to his health insurance. A hearing was requested for the failure to calculate the correct average weekly wage. The Administrative Law Judge agreed with Groover and recalculated his average weekly wage to include the benefits. This increased the amount of his weekly indemnity benefits. The Full Board reversed because the reimbursements "do not result in the receipt of funds which can be spent by the recipient."[91] The Superior Court affirmed the Full Board's decision. The Court of Appeals affirmed, writing that "we have found no reported Georgia judicial decision so broadly construing the **O.C.G.A. Section 34-9-260** definition of 'average weekly wage' to encompass an employer's direct payment to an insurance provider for health benefits."[92] The court also addressed the conflict between the Board Rule and the statute, stating "[A]lthough the wording of a Board Rule has significance, such language cannot be used to supersede or replace express statutory language to the contrary."[93]

---

[89] <u>Pizza Hut Delivery v. Blackwell</u>, 204 Ga. App. 112, 418 S.E.2d 639 (1992).

[90] 241 Ga. App. 791, 527 S.E.2d 639 (2000).

[91] <u>Id</u>. at 641.

[92] <u>Id</u>.

[93] Citing <u>Blackwell</u>, *supra*, 204 Ga. App.

There are two types of indemnity benefits under Georgia's worker's compensation system:

> *   Temporary Total Disability (TTD) and
> *   Temporary Partial Disability (TPD).

Temporary Total Disability (TTD) benefits are due when the injured worker has been totally disabled by the authorized treating physician for more than seven (7) days. **O.C.G.A. Section 34-9-261** as of July 1, 2014, provides:

> "While the disability to work resulting from an injury is temporarily total, the employer shall pay or cause to be paid to the employee a weekly benefit equal to two-thirds of the employees average weekly wage but not more than $525.00 per week nor less than $50.00 per week . . ."

An injured employee is not eligible for these benefits unless and until he/she has been disabled by the authorized treating physician for more than seven (7) days.[94] According to Board Rule 220(b), "Entitlement to benefits for the first seven days of disability, or any part thereof, requires 21 consecutive days of disability. The employer/insurer shall pay compensation for the first seven days of disability on the 21st consecutive day."

What happens if the benefits are not paid in a timely fashion? The employer/insurer will be subjected to a penalty. There is a 15% penalty assessed onto the amount of the accrued income benefits which are late.[95] The State

---

at 112, 418 S.E.2d 639.
[94] See **O.C.G.A. Section 34-9-220.**

Board of Workers' Compensation considers payments as being made when mailed within the state to the address specified by the employee or to the address on record with the board, or when it is electronically transferred to an account specified by the injured worker.[96]

The most an injured worker can be paid in TTD benefits are currently $525.00 (as of July 1, 2014).[97] The minimum amount cannot be less than $50.00 per week.[98] Under most circumstances, these TTD benefits are capped and the injured worker can only receive them up to 400 weeks from the date of injury.[99] If the injured worker's disability is designated as "catastrophic", there is no limitation as to the number of weeks the claimant may draw compensation.[100]

What is a "catastrophic" designation? Your claim could be considered "catastrophic" if your injury involves one of the following:

* Amputation
* Severe paralysis
* Severe head injury
* Severe burns
* Blindness
* Or any other injury of a nature and severity that prevents an injured worker from being able to perform his or her prior work and any work available in substantial numbers within the national economy for which the

---

[95] **O.C.G.A. Section 34-9-221(e).**
[96] **O.C.G.A. Section 34-9-221(b).**
[97] **O.C.G.A. Section 34-9-261.**
[98] Id.
[99] Id.
[100] Id.

employee is otherwise qualified.[101]

If your injury falls in one of the first five categories, the catastrophic designation is automatic. Most of the litigation as to whether or not a claim is catastrophic centers on the filing category of "any other injury . . ." The injured worker has the burden of proofing that his injury qualifies under this category as catastrophic. The employee and his attorney will often have to provide very extensive medical narratives and opinions, as well as testimony from a vocational expert as to the employability of the injured worker in the national economy. The employer/insurer will naturally try and counter the medical evidence with reports from their doctors and vocational expert. An award for Social Security Disability benefits can also play an important role in determining whether an injury is catastrophic. This Social Security decision that either grants or denies disability benefits shall be admissible in evidence and the Board is directed to consider it in their evaluation; however, no presumption shall be created based upon this award regarding a catastrophic designation.[102]

It is important for the attorney for the injured worker to get very clear medical evidence from your treating physicians about your work restrictions. What are you physically capable of doing? What are the limitations? Will you be on medication that could limit your ability to perform certain jobs? What kind of education / training do you possess, and will you be able to use them with your physical restrictions? The attorney also needs to have a vocational expert review your work restrictions, evaluate your education and past work history, your age, and provide an opinion as to whether or not there is work

---

[101] **O.C.G.A. Section 34-9-200.1.**
[102] **O.C.G.A. Section 34-9-200.1(g)(6)**

available in substantial numbers within the national economy, not just Georgia's economy.

Why is this important? Why do employer/insurers want to fight the catastrophic designation? One word - money! If the injured worker receives the catastrophic designation, they are eligible to receive lifetime medical treatment, as well as lifetime indemnity benefits.[103] It is important to note that a catastrophic designation is not necessarily a permanent determination.

Temporary Partial Disability (TPD) benefits are due when an employee returns to work after an injury, but is unable to earn a gross weekly wage equal to what he was earning before the accident because of his injury and work restrictions.[104] Under the statute, the employer/insurer are to pay the injured worker 2/3 of the difference between the average weekly wage before the injury and the wage earned upon the worker's return. As of July 1, 2014, the maximum amount of the TPD benefits to be paid is $350.00 per week.[105]

For example:

> The injured worker's average weekly wage in the 13 weeks immediately preceding the on the job injury is $600.00 per week. He is totally disabled for a period of time and receives Temporary Total Disability (TTD) benefits in the amount of $400.00 per week.
> After a period of time, the authorized treating physician (ATP) releases the injured worker to light

---

[103] **O.C.G.A. Section 34-9-261.**
[104] **O.C.G.A. Section 34-9-262.**
[105] Id.

duty work and the employer has light duty work available within the doctor's restrictions. However, the injured worker is not able to work as many hours as he was pre-injury, so he earns less money. Assume he only earns $300.00 per week after he returns to work. The difference in pre-injury wage ($600.00) and post-injury return to work ($300.00) is $300.00. The employer/insurer must pay the injured worker TPD benefits of $200.00 (which is 2/3 of the $300.00 difference).

Going back to work with light duty restrictions can be the step in the right direction for most injured workers. They can use the increased money from their paycheck and have it supplemented with the TPD benefits from worker's compensation as they work to fully recover from their injuries. This is especially true in the situations where the employer values the employee and really wants to accommodate them and their restrictions.

But what happens in those situations where the employer/insurer is less than civil with the injured worker, and tries to get the employee to return to work on a light duty job - but the employer's definition of "light duty" does not necessarily agree with the authorized treating physician's view of "light duty?"

The legislature addressed this issue by passing **O.C.G.A. Section 34-9-240**. The statute is further explained by Board Rule 240. Whenever the authorized treating physician releases an injured worker to light duty work and the employee has been out of work receiving TTD benefits, the employee does not have to return to work until the employer/insurer does the following:

(1)   Prepare a detailed description of the light

duty job the employer has available for the injured worker;

(2)   Send the job description to the authorized treating physician (ATP) for his/her review. If the ATP believes the employee CANNOT perform the job, then the employee does not have to attempt it and the employer/insurer must continue paying TTD benefits. If the ATP believes the injured work CAN perform the light duty job, then the employer/insurer must take additional steps;

(3)   The employer/insurer must send the injured worker a WC-240 Form to the injured worker and his/her attorney. The employer/insurer must attach a copy of the job description that was reviewed and approved by the ATP. The form must be sent to the injured worker and his/her attorney at least ten (10) days prior to the date the employee is expected to return to work.

(4)   If the employee refuses to attempt the light duty job, the employer/insurer can suspend payment of income benefits effective the date the injured worker is supposed to return to work.

(5)   If the employee attempts the light duty job, the law provides a trial period for the worker: (a) If the employee attempts to perform the job and works for eight (8) cumulative hours or one scheduled work day, whichever is greater, but works less

than fifteen (15) working days, then the
weekly TTD benefits must be recommenced
immediately. The employer/insurer has to
request a hearing to suspend benefits if they
so desire. (b) If the employee attempts the
job but works less than one scheduled work
day or less than eight (8) cumulative hours,
whichever is greater, or more than fifteen
(15) working days, then the weekly TTD
benefits can be suspended. The employee
would have to ask for a hearing to have
benefits reinstated, and the employee has the
burden of proving a good-faith effort in
attempting the job.

The better practice is to make sure the employer/insurer
comply with the requirements of **O.C.G.A. Section 34-9-
240** and Board Rule 240 before you attempt a light duty
job.

Please note that TPD benefits are also not designed to
continue indefinitely. The underlying purpose of Georgia's
workers' compensation system is to get the injured worker
back into the workforce as quickly as possible. TPD
benefits are limited to a maximum of 350 weeks from the
date of the injury.[106]

(2)   **Medical Benefits**:

One of the mainstays of workers' compensation insurance
is that there will be timely, reliable medical care available
for injured workers. According to the Act, the
employer/insurer are required to furnish the employee

---

[106] Id.

"such medical, surgical, and hospital care and other treatment,

items, and services which are prescribed by a licensed physician, including medical and surgical supplies, artificial members, and prosthetic devices and aids damaged or destroyed in a compensable accident, which in the judgment of the State Board of Workers' Compensation shall be reasonably required and appear likely to effect a cure, give relief, or restore the employee to suitable employment."[107] Further, the medical treatment/expenses must be reasonable and customary, and prescribed by the authorized treating physician.[108]

How does an injured worker select an "authorized treating physician?" Every employer that is subject to the Act must post a panel of physicians from which the employee may select their treating physician.[109] There are two types of "panels" - traditional and conformed, and a third variation - a Managed Care Organization (MCO).

Under current law, the traditional panel must:

(1)   Have at least six (6) "unassociated" physicians or professional associations of physicians who are close in proximity for the injured worker;

(2)   At least one of the physicians must be an orthopedic surgeon;

---

[107] **O.C.G.A. Section 34-9-200(a).**
[108] Id.
[109] **O.C.G.A. Section 34-9-201.**

(3) No more than two of the six physicians can be an industrial clinic;

(4) According to Board Rule 201(a), one of the six physicians must be a minority physician. The term "minority" is defined as "a group which has been subjected to prejudice based on race, color, sex, handicap or national origin, including, but not limited to Black Americans, Hispanic Americans, Native Americans or Asian Americans." It is important to note that the Board Rule immediately contradicts its previous "requirements" by noting the "[F]ailure to include one minority physician on the panel does not necessarily render the panel invalid."[110]

The employer is required to post the panel of doctors in prominent places upon the business premises, usually in a break room or near a time clock.[111] The employer is also charged with the responsibility of making sure the employee understands the "function of the panel" and the "employee's right to select a physician" from the panel, as well as being required to give assistance to the employee to contact the physicians on the panel.[112] With a "traditional panel", once the employee selects the physician to provide treatment, then this physician is designated as the "authorized treating physician."[113] With a "traditional"

---

[110] Board Rule 201(a) and **O.C.G.A. Section 34-9-201**

[111] **O.C.G.A. Section 34-9-201(c)**

[112] Id.

[113] **O.C.G.A. Section 34-9-201**

panel, the employee is allowed to make a onetime change from the authorized treating physician to another doctor on the panel of physicians.[114]

A "Conformed Panel of Physicians" must have at least ten physicians or professional associations of doctors that are reasonably accessible to the injured worker.[115] The list can also have general surgeons and chiropractors listed on it.[116] The ten physicians or groups of physicians cannot be associated.[117] The Board also requires that at least one of the ten be a minority physician.[118]

A Managed Care Organization (MCO) is a "plan certified by the Board that provides for the delivery and management of treatment to injured employees under the Georgia Workers' Compensation Act."[119] The employer is required to post notices about the MCO in prominent places around the workplace and make efforts to insure the employee understands how the MCO works.[120]

What happens if an employer fails to comply with the law and does not post a panel of physicians, or in the alternative, posts a panel that is not in compliance with **O.C.G.A. Section 34-9-201** and Board Rule 201? The employee is free to select the physician of their choice to provide treatment and the employer/insurer has to pay for it.[121] The physician selected becomes the authorized

---

[114] **O.C.G.A. Section 34-9-201(b)(1)**

[115] **O.C.G.A. Section 34-9-201(b)(2)** and Board Rule 201(b)(2)

[116] Board Rule 201(b)(2)

[117] Id.

[118] Id.

[119] **O.C.G.A. Section 34-9-201(a)(3)**

[120] **O.C.G.A. Section 34-9-201(c)**

[121] **O.C.G.A. Section 34-9-201(f)**

treating physician. Once this physician is selected, the employee may make a one time change to another physician without employer approval or approval of the Board.[122]

When an authorized treating physician is selected by the injured worked, this physician may refer to other doctors and physicians for "specialized" testing or treatment. However, these physicians may not refer to any other doctors as only the authorized treating physician is vested with this power. However, if the authorized treating physician (ATP) agrees with the specialist's referral, the ATP may concur and refer to this specialist.[123]

What happens if the employee is injured and needs emergency medical attention? Will the emergency room visit be covered if the hospital is not one of the "physicians" on the panel of physicians? The emergency visit will be covered as long as the emergency "exists"; once the emergency is over, the employee is required to comply with the panel of physician requirements.[124]

Another problem can arise when the authorized treating physician (ATP) refuses to treat the injured worker. This can happen in two ways:

> (1) The ATP refuses to provide treatment to the injured worker; or

> (2) The ATP releases the injured worker from his care.

---

[122] Board Rule 201(c)
[123] **O.C.G.A. Section 34-9-201(b)(1) and (2)**
[124] **O.C.G.A. Section 34-9-201(d)**

In (1), the employee must produce evidence that the ATP would not see him and refused to schedule an appointment. In (2), the situation often arises when the ATP dismisses the employee from his care and opines that the worker does not need any more treatment. If the injured worker can demonstrate that he is in need of care despite the ATP's dismissal, then the employer/insurer may be liable for continuing treatment with a doctor of the employee's choosing.[125]

If the employer/insurer have controverted the entire claim - meaning they are denying that the accident and injury arose out of and in the course and scope of employment - and the claim is later accepted voluntarily or the Board finds the claim compensable, the medical care the injured worker has received can be claimed as authorized and submitted to the employer/insurer for payment. The treating physician becomes the ATP, and the injured worker is entitled to a one-time change to a physician of their choice.

Assuming the panel of physicians is valid under Georgia law, and the employee has already exercised his/her "one time change" to another doctor on the panel, how can an injured worker change physicians again? There may be a personality conflict between the patient and the doctor. The doctor may have a horrible bed-side manner and does not listen to the injured worker or he may consider the worker's complaints as whining or complaining. In this doctor-patient relationship, with that kind of distrust or poor communication, it is certainly not in the patient's best interest to continue treating with that physician. There are

---

[125] Vulcan Materials Company v. Pritchett, 227 Ga. App. 530, 489 S.E.2d 558, at 560, citing Bel Arbor Nursing Home v. Johnson, 192 Ga. App. 454, 385 S.E.2d 315 (1989).

two ways this change can be effectuated:

(1)   By agreement with the employer/insurer; or

(2)   By filing a Motion to Change Physicians with the State Board of Workers' Compensation.

If a Motion to Change Physicians is filed by either the injured worker or the employer/insurer, the Board will look at the following factors when it considers granting or rejecting the request for a change:

- Proximity of physician's office to employee's residence
- Accessibility of physician to employee
- Excessive/redundant performance of medical procedures
- Necessity for specialized medical car
- Language barrier
- Referral by authorized physician
- Noncompliance of physician with Board Rules and procedures
- Panel of physicians
- Duration of treatment without appreciable improvement
- Number of prior treating physicians
- Prior requests for change of physician/treatment
- Employee released to normal duty work by current authorized treating physician
- Current physician indicates nothing more to offer[126]

---

[126] Board Rule 200(b)(2)

Medical expenses and other treatment costs for injured workers within the workers' compensation system are supposed to be paid by the employer or insurer within 30 days of receiving the bill.[127] Health care providers are not supposed to bill the injured worker for the cost of the medical care.[128] The medical provider must submit the charges to the employer/insurer for payment within one year of the date of service.[129] The medical bills are limited to "the usual, customary, and reasonable charges as found by the Board pursuant to **O.C.G.A. Section 34-9-205**."[130] All bills submitted to the employer/insurer for payment by the health care providers must be submitted on proper Board forms, as "[N]o physician, hospital, or any other provider of services shall be entitled to collect any fee unless reports required by the board have been made."[131]

It is important to note that all health care providers must bill according to a fee schedule set up by the Board. Their liability for bills "shall be limited to such charges as prevail in the State of Georgia for similar treatment of injured persons of a like standard of living when such treatment is paid for by the injured persons."[132]

---

[127] **O.C.G.A. Section 34-9-203**
[128] **O.C.G.A. Section 34-9-205(b)**
[129] Board Rule 203(b)(1)
[130] Board Rule 203(a)
[131] **O.C.G.A. Section 34-9-205(a)**
[132] **O.C.G.A. Section 34-9-203** and Board Rule 203.

For example:

A hospital may charge $200.00 for an x-ray.
The fee schedule may limit the x-ray to $75.00.
The hospital will be paid $75.00 by the employer/insurer.
The hospital cannot bill the employee for the excess
amount of the bill - $125.00, as this amount must be written
off.

Will I ever be able to see a doctor of my choice and make
the employer/insurer pay for it? This is a question we are
often asked. The simple answer is - it depends. If an
employee has received any weekly indemnity benefits for
his on the job injury "and within 120 days of receipt of any
income benefits, [he] shall have the right to one
examination at a reasonable time and place, within this
state or within 50 miles of the employee's residence, by a
duly qualified physician or surgeon designated by the
employee and to be paid for by the employer."[133] These
examinations shall include "physical, psychiatric and
psychological examinations" and it "shall also include
reasonable and necessary testing as ordered by the
examining physician."[134] It is also important to note the
employer/insurer may require the employee to attend a
second opinion with a doctor of the employer/insurer's
choosing for a second opinion.[135]

When an employee has sustained an injury and the injury
has been accepted by the employer/insurer has

---

[133] **O.C.G.A. Section 34-9-202(e)**
[134] Board Rule 202
[135] **O.C.G.A. Section 34-9-202(a)(b) and (c)**

compensable, the employee may - under certain circumstances - be entitled to "reasonable and necessary rehabilitation services."[136] If the injury is catastrophic "the employer shall furnish the employee entitled to benefits under this chapter with reasonable and necessary rehabilitation services."[137] Within 48 hours of the injury being accepted as compensable and catastrophic, the employer/insurer must appoint a rehabilitation supplier and is required to file a Form WC-R1 with the State Board, along with the Employer's First Report of Injury form or within 15 days of notification that rehabilitation is necessary.[138]

As you might imagine, the costs of hiring a rehabilitation supplier and providing rehabilitation benefits to the injured worker can get very expensive for the employer/insurer. Every rehab supplier that handles workers' compensation claims in this state must be certified or licensed and registered with the State Board.[139] Generally, rehabilitation benefits can include:

- a vocational assessment and evaluation
- vocational planning and training
- possible advanced education
- home or vehicle modifications to aid the injured worker

One benefit often over-looked by injured workers is their right to receive reimbursement for mileage to and from their medical appointments.[140] This even includes trips to

---

[136] **O.C.G.A. Section 34-9-200.1(a)**
[137] Id.
[138] Board Rule 200.1(a)(2)
[139] Board Rule 200.1(f)
[140] Board Rule 203(e)

get prescriptions filled. We provide our clients with a form that helps them to catalog each trip. This form includes the date the trip was taken, the purpose of the trip, and the number of round trip miles.

In addition, any charges for parking are also reimbursable expenses.

(3)   **Permanent Partial Disability (PPD) Benefits**

Under Georgia's Workers' Compensation Act, there are three (3) types of PPD benefits:

(1)   Loss of a specific scheduled member (e.g., the worker loses a thumb);

(2)   Loss of use of a specific scheduled member (e.g., the worker's thumb is crushed and it is essentially non-functioning); or

(3)   an impairment to the body as a whole.[141]

When an injured worker reaches "maximum medical improvement " or (MMI) - essentially the authorized treating physician opines that the employee has recovered as well as he ever will for the injuries - the ATP will perform a disability evaluation to determine the employee's PPD rating. In order for a worker to have an injury that qualifies for PPD payments, it has to be "disability partial in character bu permanent in quality resulting from loss of use."[142] Georgia uses the "AMA Guide to the Evaluation of Permanent Impairment, 5th Edition."[143]

---

[141] **O.C.G.A. Section 34-9-263(a)**
[142] Id.
[143] **O.C.G.A. Section 34-9-263(d)**

When the ATP performs the disability evaluation, he/she will assign a percentage of impairment according to the AMA Guide.

For example: The injured worker severely injures his shoulder requiring him to undergo surgical repair. Post-surgery, he actively participates in physical therapy to regain some strength, range of motion, and flexibility in the shoulder. However, despite the ATP's best efforts, and well as the injured worker's, he will never regain 100% of his shoulder. The doctor must perform a PPD evaluation using the AMA Guides to determine the employee's percentage of disability.

The ATP might assign the following:

   15% PPD rating to the Upper Extremity
   7 % PPD rating to the Body as a Whole

   Based upon this PPD, the Employer/Insurer must pay an additional sum of money to the injured worker.

Please note: The Employer/Insurer are not required to pay PPD benefits to the injured worker as long as he/she is entitled to TTD or TPD benefits for the accident in issue.[144]

---

[144] **O.C.G.A. Section 34-9-263(b)(2)**

Georgia has a "schedule" or list that sets forth the number of weeks benefits must be paid for the total loss or loss of use of various parts of the human anatomy:[145]

Bodily Loss	Maximum Weeks
(1) Arm	225
(2) Leg	225
(3) Hand	160
(4) Foot	135
(5) Thumb	60
(6) Index Finger	40
(7) Middle Finger	35
(8) Ring Finger	30
(9) Little Finger	25
(10) Great Toe	30
(11) Any toe other than the great toe	20
(12) Loss of hearing, traumatic	
One ear	75
Both ears	150
(13) Loss of vision of one eye	150
(14) Disability to the body as a whole	300

Under the AMA Guide, impairment ratings to the neck, back or spine must be stated as a whole person impairment rating.

---

[145] **O.C.G.A. Section 34-9-263(c)**

In the previous example:

Assume the ATP assigned the following ratings:

15% to the upper extremity (UE)
7% to the body as a whole (BAW)

The PPD would be calculated as follows:

Assume the injured worker's TTD rate was $525.00. The PPD calculation would be as follows:

15% to the UE x 225 weeks x $525.00 = $17,718.75
7% to the BAW x 300 weeks x $525.00 - $11,025.00

The injured worker would be entitled to the higher of the two ratings.[146] In this example, he would choose the 15% to the UE as it equals $17,718.75.

There may be accidents where a worker sustains injuries to multiple body parts and the ATP assigns a series of PPD ratings. The Georgia Court of Appeals has ruled that under these circumstances, the injured worker is entitled to an award of PPD benefits for each of these PPD ratings.[147]

---

[146] Holcombe v. Fireman's Fund Ins. Co., 102 Ga. App. 587, 116 S.E.2d 891 (1960).
[147] N.G. Gilbert Corp. v. Cash, 181 Ga. App. 775, 353 S.E.2d 840 (1987).

CHAPTER 5:
DEATH BENEFITS

CHAPTER 5 - DEATH BENEFITS

Sometimes injuries at work are so extraordinary that they lead to the death of the employee immediately, or after extensive medical intervention. These can be far-ranging episodes from accidents - such as a fall from a high scaffolding, to an injury while operating machinery, or in a car wreck while in the course and scope of employment. Regardless of what happens in the accident, Georgia's workers' compensation system is different from other types of civil claims. The law recognizes that people who rely on the worker's income and support will suddenly be at a complete loss. Money to pay for rent, food, routine electrical and other utility bills has evaporated. The survivors need money, and they need it quickly.

When someone dies outside of a work environment, (for example: in a car wreck), the surviving spouse and/or children can file a lawsuit against the parties responsible for the death. However, the lawsuit, like most civil litigation, could take years to conclude either through a settlement or verdict. During the pending action, the spouse might have to survive on any life insurance proceeds, or any other savings the family might have. Under those conditions, it can become very difficult on the spouse to make ends meet. Georgia's workers' compensation system recognized these issues, so survivor benefits were established and these benefits should begin relatively quickly.

The employer/insurer may have continuing obligations - even after an employee's death. The first requires the employer/insurer to cover any medical expenses the injured worker incurred due to treatment rendered to him/her before the death.[148] Further, the Act requires the employer to "pay the reasonable expenses of the employee's burial not to exceed $7,500.00.

- **Who is entitled to receive Death Benefits?**

If the employee died without any dependents, then believe it or not, the employer/insurer's obligations end after payment of the medical and burial. The only other payment the employer/insurer must make would be a one time payment to the State Board of Workers' Compensation one half of the benefits that would be due if the employee died with a dependent or dependents, or $10,000.00 - whichever is **less**.[149]

If the employee did leave dependents, then one must classify which category of dependency exists. Georgia law sets forth two (2) classes of dependents:

(1)   Total and
(2)   Partial.

Total dependency occurs when a person is completely dependent upon the income for livelihood as made by the deceased employee, or someone who is designated as totally dependent as a matter of law in Georgia. An example of this second classification is a minor child (one that is under the age of 18).

Partial dependency is when a person depends on some contribution(s) from the deceased person to help support their livelihood.

---

[148] O.C.G.A. Section 34-9-265(b)(1)
[149] O.C.G.A. Section 34-9-265(f)

From a lot of experience with these claims, we have found it very difficult for the insurance companies to prove a dependent is *partially* dependent instead of *totally* dependent. Especially in this economy, so many clients are living paycheck to paycheck and they often do not have a bank account. They will immediately cash their checks so they can pay for their living expenses. If a dependent testifies that they were totally dependent on the deceased employee for their living expenses, the employer/insurer finds it very difficult to counteract this testimony as there is no paper trail to refute it.

The Workers' Compensation Act makes a conclusive presumption that a spouse is totally dependent on the deceased employee. The only exception is if the surviving spouse was living separately from the deceased worker for a period of ninety (90) days immediately preceding the accident (not the death) that resulted in the death of the employee.[150]

The Act also makes a conclusive presumption that the deceased employee's children are totally dependent.[151] However, if the "child" is over that age of 18 but is not physically or mentally capable of earning a living, then the child's age does not matter.[152] It is also important to note that the definition of children includes "dependent stepchildren, legally adopted children, posthumous children, and acknowledged children born out of wedlock but **does not** include married children. (Emphasis supplied)[153] One other interesting twist is that a parent could be totally

---

[150] O.C.G.A. Section 34-9-13(b)(1)
[151] O.C.G.A. Section 34-9-13
[152] O.C.G.A. Section 34-9-13(b)(2)(B)
[153] O.C.G.A. Section 34-9-13(a)(1)

or partially dependent upon a child if it could be shown through testimony that the child contributed to the living expenses of the parent(s).

- **<u>Surviving Spouse with NO Dependents</u>**:

If the deceased worker is found to have passed within the provisions of the Georgia's Workers' Compensation Act, and only has a spouse as a dependent, that spouse can get survivor benefits of 2/3 of the employee's wage for a maximum period of 400 weeks.[154] There are a few ways the surviving spouse can lose these benefits:

- remarriage;
- cohabitation in a "meretricious relationship";
- the spouse turns 65;
- the 400 week cap on benefits is exhausted; or
- death of the surviving spouse.[155]

A meretricious relationship is defined as one in which persons of the opposite sex openly live together for a continuous period of time, and the relationship includes either sexual intercourse or the splitting of living expenses. The rationale behind cutting the benefits off for the surviving spouse is that the Act is not supposed to be a long-term social security system for most people. For the dependents of a deceased worker, it is there as a safety net to give them time to figure out how to change their financial situations to become more self-supportive, and not just rely on the State of Georgia for continuing benefits. It may take years to adjust and find ways to replace the deceased worker's income, but the State of Georgia expects people to do so.

---

[154] O.C.G.A. Section 34-9-265
[155] O.C.G.A. Section 34-9-13(e)

The Authority on Workers' Compensation

Also note that if the deceased employee was paid wage benefits for any time after this accident, but before this death, the survivor's benefits will be reduced by the number of weeks these benefits were paid.[156]

For example: The injured worker is paid for 20 weeks before after his accident, and then he subsequently dies leaving a dependent spouse. The maximum period of dependency (400 weeks) is reduced by the 20 weeks previously paid, leaving a remaining balance of potentially 380 weeks due.

- **<u>Surviving Spouse with Dependents</u>**:

When there is a spouse and children that survive the injured worker, they are entitled to be paid compensation benefits in the same amount that the injured worker would have received in wage benefits during their dependency.[157] The compensation will be equally divided among the dependents.[158] A dependent child's benefits cease when the child reaches 18 unless enrolled full time in high school, is physically or mentally incapable of earning a living, or is under the age of 22 and is a full time student or the equivalent in good standing enrolled at a post-secondary institute of higher learning.[159]

- **<u>Partial Dependents</u>**:

---

[156] O.C.G.A. Section 34-9-265(b)(4)
[157] O.C.G.A. Section 34-9-265(b)(2)
[158] O.C.G.A. Section 34-9-13(c)
[159] O.C.G.A. Section 34-9-13(c)

If the deceased employee is survived by dependents that are only "partially dependent" on the worker's wages for living expenses at the time of the injury, then the weekly compensation amount paid to them by the employer/insurer shall be in the same proportion as the amount contributed by the deceased employee to them for their living expenses.[160]

For example:
The injured worker provided 60% of the living expenses for the dependents out of his wages. The employer/insurer would be required to pay partial dependency benefits equal to 60% of what the deceased employee's worker's compensation wage benefits would have been.

Assume worker's compensation benefits would have been $480.00 per week. The partial dependent would be entitled to 60% of that amount, or $288.00 per week.

Please note that if there are any dependents that are considered "total dependents" upon the deceased employee, then any "partial dependents" are not entitled to any compensation.[161]

---

[160] O.C.G.A. Section 34-9-265(b)(3)
[161] O.C.G.A. Section 34-9-13(c)

Chapter 6:
Common Workers' Compensation Defenses

Chapter 6 - Common Workers' Compensation Defenses

I have been practicing over 27 years now specializing in worker's compensation and personal injury law. I've represented insurance companies and employers, but have only represented injured victims since 1989. One thing I have learned helping more than 40,000 victims and their families is the insurance companies are ALWAYS trying to find a way to deny paying a valid claim, or at least doing what they can to decrease the value of a claim. It's what they do. They are a "for profit" business. They make money by charging premiums to keep the insurance in force and effect, by investing those dollars, and by paying injured victims LESS than they are entitled to receive whenever a claim is made.

In this chapter, I will discuss some key legal tactics that aggressive insurance companies *and their attorneys* will use to either deny or defend your claim. The most common defenses that insurance companies will use are outlined in **O.C.G.A. Section 34-9-17**.

(1)   **Horse play**

This is the "goofing off," "playing around on the clock", "not doing your job" defense. Generally, if you stop performing a benefit for your employer – something you are being paid to do – and instead you engage in some type of prank or practical joke, and you are hurt while doing it, then your workers' compensation claim is not compensable.

For example:

You engage in a game of "Nerf Gun Warfare" in your office during work hours. You and another employee decide to see who can shoot the other amongst the cubicles in your office. As you peer around your desk, your employee shoots you in the eye with one of the nerf bullets. The injury causes you to lose the sight in your eye permanently. If you were to file a claim seeking benefits under the Workers' Compensation Act here in Georgia, the employer/insurer would have a very good reason to deny your claim as they would assert the horse play defense.

(2) **Willful Misconduct**

Under the Workers' Compensation Act, this type of conduct generally includes:

a) an intentional, self-inflicted injury;
b) attempt to injure another;
c) willful failure to utilize a safety appliance; or
d) intoxication by alcohol or under the influence of marijuana or other controlled substance.

If the Board find there is sufficient evidence of willful misconduct by the employee that caused his/her injury, no matter how severe the injuries are, it will automatically fail if brought before an administrative law judge. The employer and insurer must prove the misconduct by a preponderance of the evidence. Also, if the worker is injured or killed while attempting to injure another, then workers' compensation benefits will be denied. (See **O.C.G.A. § 34-9-17(a)**)

It is also important to note that Georgia law may bar your recovery for workers' compensation benefits if you are injured or killed because you willfully refused to utilize a safety appliance.

Again, the burden of proof rests with the employer/insurer, and they must prove the following:

> (1) the employer provided a 'safety appliance;
> (2) the appliance was accessible to the employee;
> (3) the employee knew or was aware of the appliance;
> (4) the employee was instructed how to use the appliance;
> (5) the employee knew the danger of not using the appliance;
> (6) the employee willfully failed or refused to use the appliance;
> (7) there was no emergency situation; and
> (8) the failure to use the safety was the legal cause of the employee's injury

Also, if you are injured while under the influence of alcohol or drugs at the time of your work injury, you may also have a difficult time recovering benefits. Most employers have a policy in effect that requires the employee to immediately submit to a drug test after a work injury. If the test is positive for alcohol or drugs, then the employer and insurer have the burden of proving this impairment proximately caused your injury. The employer's defense will be strengthened if the alcohol test is performed within eight hours of the accident and the employee's blood alcohol concentration level is above the legal limit.

The burden of proof still must be met by the employer, and they will need to prove the following:

(1) the employee improperly consumed alcohol or drugs;

(2) that the employee was intoxicated at the time of the injury; and

(3) the accident generally would not have occurred but for the employee's intoxication

(3)   Lunch Break Defense

The Board and the Georgia courts have generally upheld the rule that if you are injured during a regularly scheduled employee break, then the claim will not be compensable. The reasoning behind this is the employee is free to use his time as he chooses, and therefore, he is not providing a direct benefit to his employer during lunch or while he is on a scheduled rest break. An exception may be arise when an employee is injured during the act of "ingress or egress" (coming or going) on the employer's premises. Another exception may occur if the employee is injured while performing an act that benefits the employer while the employee is on a scheduled lunch or rest break.

(4)   Employee Traveling To and From Work

The courts have held for a long time here in Georgia that an employee's duties begin and end at his place of employment. Typically, if an accident and injury occurs while the employee is going to or coming from work, it is typically not covered by the Workers' Compensation Act.

But there are exceptions, including the following:

(1) the employer provides the employee's transportation;

(2) the employee was performing a required act to benefit the employer while going to or coming from work;

(3) the employee was 'on-call';

(4) the employee is traveling from one employer location to another employer location;

(5) the employee was traveling to and from the employer's parking facilities

Please note that the Georgia courts have also established a 'doctrine of continuous employment.' This essentially means that if the particular employment requires overnight travel or is extended over multiple days for a business trip, the employee will be exposed to additional highway risks and hotel hazards. These risks may allow a recovery for benefits.

(5) Employee Deviates From the Course And Scope of Employment

If an employee decides to pursue some action for his own benefit or purpose rather than doing his required job duties and he is injured as a result, then the claim is usually not compensable nor covered by the Workers' Compensation Act.

For example:

The employee is asked to take the company's deposit to the bank. If he chooses to run by his home and he is injured during this deviation, the accident and injury are not typically compensable. However, once the employee's personal errand or task is complete, and he returns to his job duties, then a resulting accident and injury may be compensable. The courts have allowed for a 'slight' deviation in certain instances. The Courts have typically required the employee's deviation from his job duties to be of a 'pronounced character' before benefits are denied. Of course, each case has a different set of facts and circumstances, so it is impossible to apply a general rule as to whether or not a "deviation" will disqualify an employee from receiving workers' compensation benefits. For this reason, it is so important for every worker that is injured on the job here in Georgia to consult with an experienced workers' compensation attorney to carefully review and analyze all the facts of your accident and injury.

Chapter 7:
Can I Sue my Employer?
The Exclusive Remedy Rule

Chapter 7 –

Can I Sue my Employer? The Exclusive Remedy Rule

Another question that we consistently receive from people that are injured at work is:

"Can I sue my employer if I am injured on the job?"

We certainly understand the reasons behind this question, especially if you feel like your accident could have been prevented if your employer provided a safe working environment, or provided you with better tools or equipment. Sometimes injuries could have been prevented if the employer was proactive in maintaining their machinery and/or equipment.

But here is the simple, general answer:

No direct civil action can be filed against your employer.

Now here is the reason why:

Georgia has adopted the "exclusive remedy" doctrine. This rule prohibits an injured worker from filing a negligence lawsuit against the employer seeking money damages. Under the law, the sole, exclusive remedy for an injured worker is to file a claim for insurance benefits under the worker's compensation system.

1.   **What is the "Exclusive Remedy Doctrine?"**

This rule protects employers from civil actions or claims by employees that were injured on the job while working for the employer. In exchange for this "lawsuit" protection, the employer is legally obligated to provide specific workers' compensation benefits to the injured worker. For a listing of these benefits, please refer to Chapter 4 of this book. For more discussion regarding potential benefits for the surviving spouse/dependents for an accident/injury which results in the death of the injured worker, see Chapter 5.

Even though the "exclusive remedy doctrine" is the general rule that prohibits these civil lawsuits against the employer, there are certain exceptions. I highly recommend you call us to see if this applies to your specific claim. And please - do not delay!

2.　**Why do we have the "Exclusive Remedy Doctrine" in Georgia?**

The purpose is to protect employers in Georgia from exposure for two separate actions against them - one for workers' compensation, and the other, a civil lawsuit. If the rule was not in effect, it would be difficult for businesses to remain in Georgia with that potential financial exposure. This could result in less commerce and jobs available in the state.

3.　**What other claims might allow a separate law suit?**

While the employer is insulated from a law suit and can invoke the protections provided to them under the Workers' Compensation Act from additional lawsuits, a negligent third party does not have this shield to prevent claims. The exclusive remedy provision does not eliminate an injured worker's right to sue a negligent third party that was the proximate cause of their injuries.

For example:

You work as a delivery driver for your company. While you are on one of your delivery routes, in the course and scope of your employment, you are involved in a car wreck. As you go through an intersection with a green light, another driver blasts through the red traffic light that for his direction of travel and he plows into your car causing you significant injuries. He is cited for causing the wreck.

In this example, you can pursue a claim for worker's compensation benefits against your employer. In addition, you can file a claim against the at-fault driver and his insurance company for your personal injuries, medical bills, lost wages, and pain and suffering. This claim against the third party is not barred nor prohibited by Georgia's Worker's Compensation Act.

Please note: you cannot sue your employer for injuries and losses sustained in this wreck. As we discussed previously, the sole, exclusive remedy available to you is filing for worker's compensation benefits.

Another example:

You are using a large chipper that is designed to take limbs and brush into it's opening, and then chips these larger pieces into smaller pieces and spits it out at the other end of the machine. Your employer is a tree service. But there is a problem with the machine that you are using . . . Due to its improper design or because of a defect during its manufacturing process, the safety switch or emergency cut off system doesn't work. As a result, your shirt sleeve gets caught and it pulls your arm into the shredder. The result? You lose your arm in this horrific accident.

You are not only allowed to file a claim for worker's compensation benefits against your employer, but you are also allowed to pursue a claim against the machine's manufacturer due to the design and/or manufacturing defect.

Bottom line:

If you are hurt at work, please call me immediately to discuss all available claims to you. If you are hurt on the job because of the negligence of an independent, third party, you may be allowed to pursue not only the worker's compensation claim against your employer, but a civil action against the at fault party.

Since 1993, my law firm has recovered over half a billion dollars for our clients and their families in Georgia and the southeast. While there is a cap on the types of benefits and their amounts under our state's workers' compensation system, you typically do not have those barriers in a personal injury claim. So please do not delay in calling me to discuss the details of your claims, as well as all remedies that may be available to you.

4.   **Subrogation Claims By The Employer/Insurer:**

Here is one other important element to potential third party claims:

If an injured worker pursues a third party for the injuries they sustained while on the job, the employer/insurer may claim a right to be reimbursed from any recovery against that third party for the workers' compensation benefits they have paid. This reimbursement claim is known as "subrogation." The reason for this potential right of reimbursement is to prevent a double recovery by the injured worker for the same accident, and to reimburse the employer/insurer for the benefits they have paid.

Now just because they claim a right to be reimbursed does not mean we honor it. For years, we have taken a hard line approach to reimbursement. In fact, Georgia law requires the insurance company to prove the injured employee has been "fully and completely compensated in his/her claim against the third party."

At the end of this book, I have attached a copy of a presentation I gave at the Annual Worker's Compensation Seminar all the way back in 2002. This seminar is a gathering of all the attorneys and the judges that practice in the workers' compensation arena in Georgia. It is an honor and a privilege for any attorney to be asked to lecture on a continuing legal education topic to other attorneys, but it is the highest honor to have this opportunity extended at the annual seminar.

CONCLUSION

If you feel you have a claim against a third party for causing your accident and on-the-job injuries, please call me right away to discuss the specific facts of your accident. Please - DO NOT DELAY as it could limit or completely bar your ability to pursue your claim for benefits and evidence could be lost if not secured in a timely fashion.

CHAPTER 8:
**Employee Rights Under The
Workers' Compensation Act of Georgia**

CHAPTER 8:
Employee Rights Under The
Workers' Compensation Act of Georgia

Whenever an employee is hurt on the job, it is extremely important that the injured worker completely understand all of their rights. As a former attorney representing insurance companies on the other side of these cases, I can tell you - the insurance company will not go out of their way to educate you about your rights. In fact, as far as the insurance company is concerned, the less you know about your benefits, the better.

Remember: insurance companies are "for profit" entities. They are out to make money. They essentially do this three ways:

(1)   Collecting premiums to keep the insurance in force and effect;

(2)   Investing the premiums to earn more money; and

(3)   By hanging on to money they would ordinarily have to pay in claims. But if the injured worker is not aware of the benefit, then the insurance company will not knock on their door and voluntarily give the worker their money!

You owe it to yourself - to your family - to find out about all of your rights. One way is to educate yourself on the Workers' Compensation Act here in Georgia, along with the Board Rules interpreting/clarifying the statutes.

But please ask yourself these questions:

- Do you really want to take on your employer, the insurance company, and their lawyers by yourself?

- Will you have the time to learn about your rights when your focus should be going to the doctor and getting better?

- Will you be able to learn the rules of evidence and the procedures necessary to present your case at a hearing to an Administrative Law Judge?

- Will you know what forms you must file with the State Board of Workers' Compensation to protect your rights? And will you know what statutes of limitations (deadlines) apply to your claim and your benefits?

A second way to learn all about your rights is to consult with an attorney that specializes in workers' compensation claims here in Georgia. I'd recommend going behind the "consult" and actually hiring an attorney to protect your rights and be the buffer between you and the insurance company. However, please consult/hire an attorney that SPECIALIZES in workers' compensation claims. Any attorney can claim they "specialize" in a certain area of the law. I encourage you to do your due diligence to find out how many claims they have handled. Also look at the law firm's website. If it lists "workers' compensation" along with divorces, bankruptcies, criminal defense, and real estate closings, then you really must ask yourself how they can "specialize" in so many areas of the law. One of the subsequent chapters in the book deals with the subject of how you can select the right attorney for you and your claim.

The following is a link to the "Employee Handbook" that is prepared by the State Board of Workers' Compensation for Georgia. It is a summary of the employee's rights. I would use this as a beginning point to help educate you on your rights.

http://sbwc.georgia.gov/sites/sbwc.georgia.gov/files/relat ed_files/site_page/employee_handbook.pdf

This next link will take you to a publication by the State Board of Workers' Compensation that provides you with a summary of the benefits an injured worker can receive based upon their date of accident:

http://sbwc.georgia.gov/sites/sbwc.georgia.gov/files/relat ed_files/site_page/provisions.pdf

CHAPTER 9:
**Employer/Insurer Responsibilities
Under The Workers' Compensation
Act of Georgia**

CHAPTER 9:
Employer/Insurer Responsibilities
Under The Workers' Compensation Act of Georgia

If you are hurt at work, it is extremely important for you to completely understand all of your rights under the Workers' Compensation Act of Georgia. It is equally important for you to learn all of the insurance company's responsibilities! As stated in the preceding chapter, the insurance company will not go out of their way to make sure you are educated on their responsibilities. It does not benefit them to do this. So you can either educate yourself, or hire an attorney that specializes in workers' compensation to help you in your case. One of the subsequent chapters in this book deals with the subject of how you can select the right attorney for you and your claim.

My firm has handled over 40,000 worker's compensation, wrongful death, and personal injury claims here in Georgia. This is all we do! We do not handle divorces, criminal cases, bankruptcy claims, or real estate closings. To learn more about me and the experienced team of lawyers and case managers working in my law firm, I encourage you to visit our website.

www.GaryMartinHays.com

The site is loaded with information and so many educational videos explaining the workers' compensation system, as well as addressing some of the most common questions we receive from our clients on a daily basis. I encourage you to take some time and explore the site, watch the videos, and find out how more about us!

The following is a link to the "Employer Information" sheet that is prepared by the State Board of Workers' Compensation for Georgia. It is a summary of the employer's responsibilities. I would use this as a beginning point to help educate you on the obligations of employers under the Act.

http://sbwc.georgia.gov/employer-information

Chapter 10 –
Statutes Of Limitations for
Workers' Compensation Claims in Georgia

Workers' Compensation Claims in Georgia

One question we often receive from people that have been injured on the job is:

"How long do I have to report a work injury to my employer after the accident and injury?"

And this question is soon followed by this one:

"How much time after my accident do I have to claim my workers' compensation benefits from the employer and the insurance company?"

We certainly understand the importance of these questions and why you want, need and deserve answers right away. It is also important to note that if you do not act in a timely fashion, you could risk losing your ability to receive any medical treatment or other benefits for your work-related injuries. It is always best to call us right away to ensure you will not be denied these important benefits because you didn't act quickly enough.

1.   **Types of Limitations Periods**

      A.   Notice

If you are hurt at work here in Georgia, the workers' compensation laws require that you report the accident/injury to your employer within **30 days of the injury date**. Please note: the thirty (30) day countdown does not begin to run until you actually realize that you are injured, not necessarily from the actual date of your accident or the incident that may have caused the injury.

For example:

You are lifting boxes and you feel a "pop" in your

back. You assume it is just a strain and will get better as you don't feel much pain at the time of the popping sensation. Because you don't think it is a big deal, you don't mention it to your supervisor that day. But a few days later, you start feeling stiffness and soreness and a pain shooting down your leg. This worries you, so you report the back injury to your supervisor. In this example, the 30 day reporting requirement begins on the day you experienced the pain and when you **first had a reason to believe you suffered a work-related injury**, not the day you felt the popping sensation from lifting the boxes.

Your injury also doesn't have to be an immediate, acute incident to be covered under Georgia's workers' compensation system. An injury can also be sustained over a period of time, rather than an immediate, identifiable accident. Some injuries, such as carpal tunnel syndrome or repetitive use syndrome, occur over time and can take weeks or months to manifest to the point where the "injury" causes a worker to become disabled from performing their job. In this situation, the actual "date of injury", as well as the 30 day notice period begins to run the date the injured worker stopped being able to work due to the injury.

Who can provide the notice of the injury to the employer?

Notice of the injury can be given by the injured employee or by anyone acting as his/her "representative." For practical purposes, the injured worker can designate a person to notify the employer on their behalf, such as a spouse or family member. We often see this when the person is unable to communicate due to the severity of the injuries.

Who do you tell about the work accident and injury?

Notice of your accident and injury should be given to your immediate supervisor. For example, if the injured worker is actually a supervisor, then he must still report the injury to his/her immediate supervisor.

B.   Claims Limitations

Once the accident is reported to your supervisor or someone in management at the job site, you also have an obligation to file a written claim with the State Board of Workers' Compensation. This claim form lets the board know not only about your accident and injury, but whether or not you are seeking any type of wage or medical benefits. There are different limitation periods that apply during the different stages of a claim. In this chapter, we will review some of the most common claims limitations. But please remember – this is just for illustration purposes as laws constantly change, and nothing can replace speaking with an attorney experienced in workers' compensation here in Georgia to determine what specific limitations may apply to your case.

When must you file a claim with the Board?

In general, an injured worker has **one year** from the date of the accident to file a claim with the State Board.

> For example:
> You are hurt at work and you immediately report the accident and injury to your immediate supervisor. You never receive any medical treatment or workers' compensation income benefits from the employer/insurer for your injuries.

But 6 months later, the problem becomes more annoying and you decide to pursue treatment for your injuries. However, the employer refuses to authorize any medical treatment because of the time that has passed since your injury.

Does the statute of limitations prevent you from filing a written claim with the State Board and seeking medical benefits from the employer?

NO! You timely reported the accident and injury to your employer. Even though you did not ask to have medical treatment initially for your injury, you are still well within the one year limitation period for filing the written claim with the Board.

You can also file Notice with the State Board within one (1) year from the last date of medical treatment!

If you never receive any wage benefits from the employer/insurer for your on the job injuries, this is still not a bar for you to be able to receive medical treatment. However, to preserve your claim, **you must treat with the workers' compensation doctors at least one (1) time per year** to keep your medical claims open and to prevent them from being barred by the limitations period.

For example:

You are treating with the workers' compensation doctor for the on the job injuries. However, you are able to work as the employer is able to accommodate the work restrictions. Since you are working, you have not received any income benefits.

Assume the last appointment with your workers' compensation doctor was on May 23, 2012, when the doctor released you from his care. On June 5, 2013, you call to make an appointment with your treating doctor because your injuries are once again bothering you. But when you call, the doctor's office tells you that the workers' compensation insurer has DENIED payment for any further treatment.

Is your claim barred by the statute of limitations from filing a written claim with the State Board?

YES!

Why? Because you were not treated by the workers' compensation doctor in over a year since your last appointment date, your claim is barred due to the limitations period. If you had requested the appointment on May 22, 2013, the claim for medical treatment would not have been barred, as this request would have been made BEFORE the one year limitation's period.

Please note: one other factor could affect the limitations period . . . .

You can also file the Notice with the State Board within two (2) years from the date of payment of your last income benefit.

It is extremely important to understand that there is a time limitation on filing a written claim for workers' compensation income benefits. You must file your written claim for income benefits within two (2) years of the last receipt of workers' compensation income benefits for the same work injury.

> For example:
> You hurt your back at work on May 23, 2010. The
> doctor puts you on light duty restrictions. However,
> your employer cannot offer suitable light duty work,
> so you are paid workers' compensation wage
> benefits. You continue to receive these wage checks
> and you receive medical treatment until your
> employer decides to offer you suitable light duty
> work. On December 15, 2010, you return to work
> at the warehouse and the employer/insurer stop your
> weekly wage benefits. You are able to work this
> light duty job but you continue to see the workers'
> compensation doctor for treatment. Over time, your
> back injury worsens. On December 16, 2012, your
> authorized treating physician places you on Total
> Disability meaning you cannot work at all due to
> your back pain.
>
> Are you entitled to workers' compensation wage
> benefits on December 16, 2012?
>
> Typically, the answer is <u>NO</u> because you have not
> received any income benefit payments for the same
> work injury in over two years - since December 15,
> 2010.

Please note: there are some exceptions to this rule, so it is
highly recommended that you ALWAYS consult an
attorney that is experienced in the workers' compensation
arena to determine your rights under Georgia law. Please -
DO NOT DELAY as the failure to act could limit or
completely bar your ability to pursue and receive your
benefits.

CHAPTER 11:
What Can I Expect At A Hearing

CHAPTER 11 - What Can I Expect At A Hearing

We have all seen the television show. The judge looks down at the counsel table. He moves his reading glasses further down his nose so he can clearly see the attorney sitting at the desk, writing something on a note pad. He speaks with his slow, southern drawl "Mr. Finch, you may proceed with your opening statement to the jury." The attorney slowly rises from his chair. He looks over at his client sitting next too him. He puts his hand on her shoulder and tells her "It's going to be ok." He buttons his coat and then walks around the table. He stops in front of the wooden rail and sees 12 people sitting in front of him, all slightly leaning forward, ready for him to tell them the story of what happened to his client. He begins . . . "Your Honor, Ladies & Gentlemen of the jury . . . "

The first thing an injured worker needs to understand about the workers' compensation is that there are NO juries. Your case will be presented to an Administrative Law Judge, not a jury. There are no opening statements, nor closing arguments. And it is a rare occasion when the Judge rules from the bench on the date of the hearing.

So now we know what **does not** happen. Let's break down what **does** . . .

- ## Hearing Request

To file a request for a hearing, the party must file a WC-14 Notice Of Claim Form with the State Board of Workers' Compensation. The form is essentially broken down into six (6) parts:

(1)   Claim Identification:

This section identifies the Employee, their social security number, and the date of injury.

(2)   <u>Claim information</u>:

In this section, one must list and identify the employee, the employer, and the insurance company. Addresses, phone numbers and emails are also listed.

(3)   <u>Hearing/Mediation Issues</u>:

This section requires the party that is requesting the hearing to specifically list what issues need to be resolved at a hearing or mediation.

For example:

A worker is injured on the job in the course and scope of his employment on July 1, 2015. He is totally disabled for a month due to his injuries and has not returned to work. The insurance company for the employer has not yet started his wage benefits nor pay for his medical benefits.

The attorney requesting the hearing would list the following:

<u>X</u>   TTD benefits from 07/01/15 and continuing.

X   Medical Benefits:
Hospital ER
Orthopedist
Physical Therapy
Dates of service and balances to be
supplemented.

X   Late-Payment Penalties/Assessed Attorney's
Fees
X   34-9-221(e)
X   34-9-108(b)(1)
X   34-9-108(b)(2)

If a mediation is requested, the filing party
must specify which issues are ripe for
mediation.

(4)   <u>Affirmation Of Filing Party</u>

This section affirms that the party (or their
representative that is filing the request for
hearing) certifies that the information
contained in the hearing request is true and
correct.

(5)   <u>Entry Of Appearance</u>

This section certifies that the attorney that is
handling the claim on behalf of the
designated party has a signed contract with
that party that is in compliance with the Act
and Board Rules.

(6)   <u>Certificate Of Service</u>

The person filing the hearing request certifies that he/she has sent a copy to all parties named in the WC-14 Hearing / Mediation Request, along with a copy to the State Board for filing.

A hearing will generally be **scheduled** within 60 days after the WC-14 Request For Hearing is filed with the Board. However, this does not necessarily mean the hearing will take place on that date. It seems to be the general practice that the board will allow either party to request a continuance if it is the first time the hearing appears on the calendar.

- **Discovery Period**

Whenever either side requests a hearing, the worker's compensation act allows the parties to conduct "discovery" regarding the case from the opposing party. Discovery procedures within the workers' compensation arena are governed by the Civil Practice Act of Georgia.[162] According to Board Rules, "[D]iscovery conducted pursuant to the Civil Practice Act shall only be permitted after a hearing has been requested in the claim, or as otherwise specified in these rules, or by agreement of the attorneys or permitted by an Administrative Law Judge or the Board."[163]
Discovery is essentially the process of gathering important, relevant information regarding the claims of the employee, or the defenses of the employer/insurer.

It is important to note that some exchange of documents can occur prior to a hearing request:

---

[162] O.C.G.A. Section 34-9-102(d)
[163] Board Rule 102(f)(2)

- The injured employee must sign a WC-207 Medical Authorization whenever he/she submits a claim for compensation.[164] This medical release allows the employer/insurer to get a copy of the claimant's medical records from any doctor the employee has seen, not just the treating physicians for the on-the-job injury.

- All parties are entitled to receive from each other any documents that are specified in the Form WC-102 Requests For Documents To Parties.[165] When this form is sent to the opposing party, documents must be produced, including Board Forms, wage records, medical reports, job descriptions, etc. This request can be sent prior to or subsequent to a hearing request.

- The employer/insurer can also compel an employee that is seeking workers' compensation benefits to attend a medical examination at reasonable times and places while the claim is ongoing.[166]

The following items are also sent to the opposing party when a hearing has been requested:

- **<u>Interrogatories:</u>**

These are a series of questions which must be answered under oath by the party to whom

---

[164] O.C.G.A. Section 34-9-207
[165] Board Rule 102(f)(1)
[166] O.C.G.A. Section 34-9-202(a).

they are directed.

- **Request For Production Of Documents:**

This is a formal notice to produce documents within the custody and control of the party to whom they are directed.

- **Requests To Admit:**

This is a series of questions directed to a party that asks them to either "admit" the statement, "deny" the statement, or state that they do not have enough information available to them to either admit nor deny. This is a low cost, effective way to find out the facts to which all parties agree so one can focus on the issues in dispute.

- **Deposition:**

This is when a party can question witnesses to a claim, under oath, to find out what that person knows prior to a hearing. Their testimony is usually transcribed by a court reporter.

- **Hearing:**

Once the WC-14 hearing request is filed, the State Board of Workers' Compensation will assign the claim to one of the administrative law judges and the claim will be set for a hearing date. The hearing will be held at the location listed on the hearing notice.

There are no juries in any workers' compensation hearing. The case will be heard by an administrative law judge in the form of a "bench trial." When the judge calls the case, the attorneys and parties will sit and tables in front of the judge. The judge will then ask the attorneys for the parties to concisely state the issues to be decided by him/her in the hearing. A brief statement of either sides contentions are made. The judge will then ask the court reporter to start recording the proceedings and he/she will then state the reason for the hearing, as well as identify all parties present. The party with the burden of proof goes first in the hearing.

For example:

If you were injured on the job and the employer/insurer is refusing to provide a benefit to you, such as paying you your weekly worker's compensation check, then you have the burden of proving that you are eligible to receive those benefits.

Or, the employer/insurer may claim that you are receiving worker's compensation checks, but you have experienced a change in condition for the better. So they are asking the judge to discontinue benefits to you because the reason for your current disability is not due to injuries sustained on the job, but for some reason completely unrelated to your on the job injury.

The attorneys will call the witnesses they feel are necessary to prove their case. The other side is given the opportunity to ask questions of the witnesses if they desire. All witnesses will be sworn in by the court reporter and must tell the truth subject to perjury charges if they fail to testify truthfully. Documents may also be tendered into evidence, such as medical records, bills, disability slips, or lost wage information. At the conclusion of the hearing, if either side has requested an assessment of attorneys' fees because the claim has been prosecuted or defended in bad faith, the attorney may present evidence of the conduct as well as evidence of the reasonable value of their fees. When the hearing is completed, the judge will likely close the record, meaning no additional evidence will be submitted nor reviewed.

It is important to note that - absent extraordinary circumstances - the judge will not issue his/her decision on the date of the hearing. The judge will allow the attorneys to present briefs on the hearing to summarize their positions and comment on the evidence introduced at the hearing. After reviewing the hearing transcript and the briefs, and considering all of the evidence, the judge will issue the hearing decision setting forth the Findings of Fact and Conclusions of Law.

Either side has the option of appealing a decision from the Administrative Law Judge. If an appeal is filed, it will be heard by the Full Board at the State Board of Workers' Compensation.

Some additional notes regarding a workers' compensation hearing:

- You should always tell the truth! You are sworn in by the judge or the court reporter and your testimony is under oath.

- Answer the questions that are asked of you truthfully, politely, and directly.

- Dress appropriately when attending the hearing to show respect to the Judge, as well as to the justice system. This is an important day and it should be treated accordingly.

- Please make sure you listen and give the judge,

the attorneys, and any witnesses your full, undivided attention.

- It is important to make sure you understand a question before you answer. If you do not understand the question, please let the person asking you the question know this. Wait for them to ask the question again or rephrase it.

- EVERY single one of the Administrative Law Judges is fair and impartial to all the parties. I assure you they will try to decide your claim based upon the evidence and the law. Always be courteous and respectful to the Judge. They deserve it.

- Understand that there are delays that are beyond your attorney's control. It may take several months before the judge issues a decision on your case. There is nothing an attorney can do to expedite the process. The judge is going to read, review and consider all the evidence before issuing the decision.

- Hearings are stressful. If it is necessary to go to a hearing over your claim, it is because there was no reasonable compromise that could be reached with the opposing side. Your attorney should discuss your claim in depth prior to the hearing so you will know the issues and points of contention that will be addressed. Also, do not be surprised if the opposing party attempts to discredit you by introducing surveillance video taken of you, or by asking you about "negative" information about you or your alleged disability.

Chapter 12:
Settlement Of The Claim

Chapter 12:   Settlement Of The Claim

Two questions I am often asked in an initial office
conference with a client are:
  (1) How long is this going to take? And
  (2) What is my case worth?

This is how I respond in most situations to these questions:

  (1) The most valuable aspect of any injured worker's
      claim for compensation is the ability to get the
      medical treatment they need paid for by the
      insurance company. In most situations, it is not in
      the best interest of the employee to attempt to settle
      their worker's compensation claim until they have
      reached maximum medical improvement. If any
      additional testing or procedures are being
      recommended by the authorized treating physician,
      you are taking a great risk by settling your claim.

      For example:

      Assume you injured your lower back at work. The
      initial doctor that evaluates you at the occupational
      clinic believes you just have a muscle strain in your
      back. He refers you to an orthopedic surgeon for an
      evaluation. The orthopedic surgeon orders an MRI
      and it confirms you have something more serious
      than a sprain as it shows you have a herniated disk
      at L3-4.

      The surgeon wants you to try physical therapy and
      epidurals to see if this will provide some relief to
      you.

You are just getting tired of the entire situation as you are only getting a low weekly compensation check, you are still hurting, and you are tired of staying at home.

Is it in your best interest to settle at this point?

I would not recommend settlement at this juncture as there are far too many unknowns. What happens if everything goes wrong that could go wrong for you medically – will you be protected? If you have settled your claim, and you eventually decide on having the surgery, how will you pay for it? Also, who will pay for your lost time from work as you are out recuperating from the surgery? And what happens if the surgery is not a success and you suffer further disability and the potential for more surgeries?

It is so important to have a full and complete understanding of your medical situation before you ever consider the possibility of settlement.

(2) And this is a perfect transition to the next question. If you don't know what the future holds for you medically, nor how much it will cost, you will never be able to truly put a settlement value on your claim. How much will your future medical bills be? How long will you be disabled? What kind of disability rating will be assigned to you?
These are just a few of the questions that should be asked and answered before anyone can arrive at what the true value of your claim will be.

Whenever you consider settling your worker's compensation claim, it should be done after a full and complete review of your medical situation and the insurance company's potential exposure. But please note: settlement in any workers' compensation claim in Georgia is always voluntary by either party. We cannot do anything as an attorney to force the Employer/Insurer to settle your claim. Also, the employer/insurer cannot force you to settle if you do not want to do so.

It is also important to understand this fact: Georgia's workers' compensation laws are not slanted in favor of the injured worker. The law severely limits not only the types of benefits you can recover, but also the amount of those benefits. If you are injured at work here in Georgia, your benefits are limited to the following:

- wages (temporary total disability (TTD) and/or temporary partial disability (TPD);
- medical benefits; and
- a permanent impairment rating (PPD).

Unfortunately, the law does not provide compensation in a fourth category so you can recover money for pain and suffering and emotional suffering. In addition, there is no right to get in front of a jury to ask them to award you a verdict of money damages as the law limits your recovery to ONLY the first three categories of benefits.

Before I had the privilege of representing injured workers, I was a defense attorney that represented employers and insurance companies on the other side of these claims. In that capacity, I would evaluate claims for settlement and make recommendations to the insurance company how much money they should ultimately pay to try and settle a workers' compensation claim. When you hire the Law Offices of Gary Martin Hays & Associates, you can have the confidence and trust in that we are evaluating your claim exactly the same way that the workers' compensation insurance company and their defense lawyers are evaluating your claim.

So how does the insurance company put a settlement value on your worker's compensation claim?

The insurance adjuster will evaluate your claim based upon the company's exposure if they have to pay any or all of the three aforementioned benefit categories.

(1)   What are they paying you in wage benefits?
Are you receiving Total Disability Benefits (TTD)? If so, in what amount?
How long do they anticipate having to pay you these benefits?
Are you receiving Temporary Partial Disability Benefits (TPD)?
If so, in what amount?
And how long do they believe they will have to pay these benefits?

For example:

You are receiving weekly TTD checks in the amount of $525.00 per week. Assume the insurance adjuster believes you will be out of work for a total of 2 years. This equals a total exposure of $54,600.00 ($525 x 104 weeks).

(2)   The adjuster will review your medical records and possibly call or write your doctor for more information on your medical situation. Assume the doctor believes you will need 7 more physical therapy visits at $100.00 per visit. Further, you may need prescriptions that total $100.00 for the next 7 weeks. The doctor does not anticipate any further medical needs past the physical therapy. The insurance company's total exposure for medical benefits would be:

$100.00 x 7 = $700
+ $100 for Prescriptions for a total of $800.00.

(3)   When you have reached maximum medical improvement (MMI), essentially when you have recovered as well as you possibly can for your injuries, the doctor will perform a disability evaluation according to the 5th Edition of the American Medical Association Guidelines.

For example:

Assume your doctor tells you that you have a 7% impairment rating (PPD) to the body as a whole, the rate is calculated as follows:

7% x 300 (300 weeks) x $525 (your TTD Rate) = $11,025.00 in additional exposure.

The total exposure can then be calculated as follows:

TTD	=	$54,600.00
Medical	=	$ 800.00
PPD	=	$11,025.00
Total Exposure		$66,425.00

Please understand: even though the insurance company's potential exposure is $66,425.00, does not necessarily mean they are willing to actually offer you a settlement in that amount. Their goal is to pay you as little as possible to resolve your case. This is further evidence as to why you need an attorney that is experienced to help you evaluate your claim, and maximum your physical and financial recovery.

O.C.G.A. Section 34-9-15 is the law that sets forth specific guidelines as to how workers' compensation claims are settled here in Georgia. When the parties have reached an agreement, a document is drafted that memorializes the settlement, and it is signed by all the parties. The settlement document is entitled 'Stipulation and Agreement.' This document may be either a "liability" or "no-liability" stipulation as it depends on whether or not the insurance company ever paid any income benefits to the employee during the claim. When the settlement agreement is presented to the board, the parties are essentially asking the State Board of Workers' Compensation to issue an Award approving the agreement. No workers' compensation settlement in Georgia is ever truly final until the State Board approves the stipulation and agreement.

Once the Board reviews the agreement and approves it, the insurance company has twenty (20) days from the day of approval to issue payment to our office. If it is not paid within that time period, then a 20% penalty is added to the total settlement amount. When the settlement agreement is approved by the State Board of Workers' Compensation, the claim is over and the claim is resolved in its entirety. The parties are legally barred by **O.C.G.A. §34-9-15** from ever amending, modifying, or changing the terms of the agreement in any manner. This is further evidence of the importance of making sure you have a complete understanding of where you are medically before you consider settlement of your claim.

CHAPTER 13:
Mediation

CHAPTER 13 - Mediation

Often times during the course of a claim an issue or several issues may arise in a workers' compensation claim that cannot be resolved by the parties. One option is to file for a hearing to have an Administrative Law Judge decide the claim after protracted litigation. This option can also be a burden on the Administrative Law Judges as their hearing calendars can become overloaded and backlogged. But the State Board of Workers' Compensation decided back in 1994 that there are times when another form of dispute resolution could be invoked. This option allows the parties to sit across the table from each other, with an independent third party acting as an intermediary, in hopes that a discussion could bring about a quicker agreement. The Board's Alternative Dispute Resolution Unit, or "ADR Unit", is an effective and efficient option to allow parties the chance to quickly resolve issues that could otherwise take months.

What is a Mediation?

Mediation is a FREE process that allows each side to come together, face to face, to address an issue or several issues in a claim that cannot be resolved by the parties alone. An independent, third party will bring the parties together in a conference to discuss the issues in dispute. He/She will hear from the attorneys their positions on the issues at this joint session. The employee and the employer/insurer may also offer their input if they desire. This is an informal session and the mediator does not require the parties to go through the hoops of introducing evidence as you would be required to do at a hearing.

Once the joint conference is complete, the parties will then be moved to different rooms. The mediator will then discuss the issues with each party individually. He/She will give them their thoughts on the problems they are trying to resolve, and will then see what solutions are available to address the issue that can be agreed to by all parties. Unlike a hearing where there is often a winner and a loser, a mediation allows the parties to decide (rather than the judge), what a fair solution to the problem can be. Mediation is non-binding, but it is an effective and efficient way to see if the parties can solve problems sooner than the costlier "later."

<u>What issues will the Board mediate</u>?

It is important to note that not all issues can be resolved at a mediation. Sometimes a hearing is the only way to resolve a dispute. The following is a list of issues the Board will typically schedule for a mediation:

(1)   Any request to change physicians;

(2)   Any request for specialized medical care / testing;

(3)   Disputes regarding the payment of a medical bill in claims that have been accepted as compensable;

(4)   Any dispute regarding suitable employment;

(5)   Disputes regarding attorney's fees (assuming the parties agree that some amount is owed);

(6)   A request by the parties to try and settle the claim;

(7)   Disputes regarding the average weekly wage of the employee;

(8)   Disputes regarding the Permanent Partial Disability (PPD) rating assigned to the injured worker;

(9)   Any issue that may arise out of the handling of a catastrophic claim.

It is important to note that the Board will not step in and try to mediate any aspect of a case that has not been accepted as compensable. The compensability of a claim occurs when the employer/insurer agree that there was an accident and injury arising out of and in the course and scope of the employee's employment and benefits are due.

How can a party ask for a Mediation?

There are a list of issues that will automatically result in the claim being referred to mediation with the ADR unit - even if a WC-14 Request For Hearing has been filed with the Board. Below is a list of the most common ways to request a Mediation:

- **Form WC200(b)**:

    This is a form that seeks a Change in Physician or a request for Additional Treatment.

- **Request for payment of medical bills**:

There are two ways this can be done:

(1)   File a WC-14 request for a hearing and specify the bills that need to be paid; or

(2)   File a Motion on a Form WC-102(g), along with supporting documentation.

- **<u>Refusal for the Employee to Accept Suitable Employment</u>**:

This is a request submitted by the Employer/Insurer that begins with them filing a Form WC-14 request for a hearing. Another method would be to file a Motion on a Form WC-102(g) along with supporting documentation.

- **<u>Disputes over attorneys' fees</u>**:

The ADR unit will consider mediating these disputes if the parties agree that fees are owed, but the only issue remaining is the amount of the fees. This can be done by filing a WC-14 request for a hearing.

- **<u>Settlement</u>**:

The attorneys will file a WC-14 request for a hearing and check the "Other" box and note that all parties agree to have a settlement mediation.

- **<u>Wage amount disputes</u>**:

If weekly checks are being paid, but there is a dispute over the amount, the WC-14 request for a hearing can be filed over this issue.

- **<u>Permanent Partial Disability (PPD) Ratings</u>**:

Disputes involving the percentage of disability an injured employee has because of the on-the-job injury may be resolved at mediation by filing a WC-14 request for a hearing.

- **<u>Disputes regarding Catastrophic claims</u>**:

  Disputes over medical treatment, medical appliances, home modifications, attendant care, or other issues can be resolved at mediation by filing a WC-14 request for a hearing.

There are so many reasons why an injured worker should consider mediation as an alternative to pursuing the issues at a hearing. But sometimes, a mediation does not result in a resolution of the issues in dispute. When appropriate, a hearing may be the only way to get a final decision on a matter.

Chapter 14:
How do I choose the best lawyer for my case?

Chapter 14 –
How do I choose the best lawyer for my case?

A question I am often asked by people is "How do I choose the best lawyer for my case?"

The hiring of a lawyer is an important decision and can make or break your case in some situations. Here are some tips you can use to help you find the attorney best suited to help you with your claim:

(1)   Find out if the attorney specializes in the area of law in which you need him or her.

        For example: If you are hurt on the job, you don't want to hire an attorney that mainly handles divorce cases or DUI cases. In my opinion, the days of an attorney handling all legal matters from divorces to real estate closings to auto accident claims are long gone. You have heard the old expression - "Jack of all trades. Master of none." I firmly believe this. Laws change constantly. It is very difficult, if not impossible, for an attorney to keep current on the latest happenings in every legal arena.

      Attorneys can claim they "specialize" in a certain area of the law, but do your due diligence to verify this. If the attorney claims to specialize in "personal injury" claims, but his/her website lists cases outside the personal injury arena like bankruptcy, or criminal defense, or collection defense matters, then there is a good chance they have not handled or do not handle a lot of cases for car wreck victims.

Workers' Compensation is a unique area of the law within which to practice here in Georgia. Not only does an attorney have to be familiar with the laws set for in the Workers' Compensation Act, but he/she must also be well versed in understanding the Board Rules. This is not an area where an attorney should practice every now and then. Specialization is key!

(2)   Find out if the attorney is recognized in your field as an expert <u>by other attorneys</u>.
        What awards or honors has the attorney received? For example, I have previously been recognized as a "Super Lawyer" in Workers' Compensation by other lawyers in Georgia. This is an honor given to only the top 5% of attorneys in the state.

        Another way to see if the attorney is respected in the field is to find out if he/she lectures to other attorneys around the state in their practice areas. I've taught other attorneys that devote a substantial portion of their practice to personal injury claims how I handle car wreck and workers' compensation claims at my law firm.

        I am also a member of the Multi-Million Dollar Advocate's Forum. This is one of the most prestigious groups of personal injury attorneys in the world. Membership is limited only to attorneys who have received a settlement or verdict of at least $2 Million Dollars.

(3)   It is also VERY important that the attorney has EXPERIENCE handling your type of claim. Find out how many cases the attorney has handled like yours. You do not want your case to be the attorney's first! For example, at the time that I am writing this book, we have helped over 35,000 injured victims and their families for cases involving serious injuries and deaths in car wrecks, worker's compensation claims, nursing home abuse, and due to defective products or drugs.

(4)   I also believe the size of the law firm matters, and not necessarily the number of attorneys the firm has. Let me explain. As attorneys, we are often in court, away from the office taking depositions, or out meeting with experts on our cases. We aren't always available to answer our client's questions. It is important for the attorney to have a knowledgeable support staff to assist you with your questions when the attorney is not available. It is also important that my attorneys and staff have continuing education in the area in which they practice.

(5)   Also find out if the law firm uses the latest in technology. At my law firm, you will not see a big law library because we don't need all of those legal books as all of our legal research is computerized. I have invested hundreds of thousand dollars in state of the art computer hardware and high tech programs specifically designed to better serve our clients needs. When you call, we can instantly access your database to tell you what has happened,

and what will be happening with your claim. This process allows us to efficiently handle your case and keep you better informed.

- ### Who NOT To Hire!

Over the years, I have provided expert advice on all of the major network affiliates in Atlanta, including ABC, CBS, FOX, NBC and the CW Network. I also have made guest appearances on CNN's Headline News and have appeared on Fox & Friends. I even hosted the only five (5) day a week legal talk show on Atlanta's CW Network, "The Gary Martin Hays Show." As a result of those appearance, I receive countless e-mails from people regarding their potential claims.

I strongly suggest you NEVER hire an attorney that contacts you out of the blue - someone who you have never called or emailed regarding your claim. The same thing applies to anyone acting on that attorney's behalf - are out there engaging in this kind of practice. We call these people "runners." The goal for these runners is to refer you to attorneys, doctors, or chiropractors to represent them. If the attorney or chiropractor is able to sign up the client, they will pay the runner a referral fee.

This practice is illegal and unethical for attorneys to be out there soliciting cases like this. This practice is called "solicitation." Further, we are ethically prohibited from paying anyone else to solicit an injured victim to hire our office. Attorneys hire these runners to do their dirty work and deny they had any knowledge this person was out soliciting cases for them.

Some runners will refer the injured person to a doctor or chiropractor who will conveniently have an attorney at the

office when they arrive for their first visit. The chiropractor will strongly recommend that the injured person sign on with this attorney or they will have to pay for all of their doctor's visits up front.
It is a racket and a scam.

What advice do I have if this happens to you? Here are a couple of suggestions:

> **First** - Get the name and phone number of the person that is calling you. Ask them what lawyer they are working with on these cases.
>
> If they deny they are working with a lawyer, ask them what doctor.
>
> As soon as you have the name of the runner, the attorney or the doctor, tell the person calling you that you appreciate the information. You are now going to call the proper authorities and they should not call you again.
>
> Hopefully, they will leave you alone after they hear this.
>
> **Second** - NEVER, NEVER, NEVER hire any attorney or doctor that will solicit you to be their client or patient. It is unprofessional, unethical and illegal for them to be doing this. Is this the kind of person you want to entrust with your medical care and your legal case?

Everything I do to market my law firm is completely within

the rules set forth by the State Bar of Georgia. I let people know that I'm here for them. If they are hurt and have a question about their rights, or the insurance company's responsibilities, I'm just a phone call or an email away.

- **Attorney's Fees & Costs**:

I have been practicing law strictly in the personal injury/workers' compensation field for over 26 years. The standard fee contract that attorneys use is called a "contingency fee contract." In layman's terms, this means (or SHOULD mean) that there are NO attorney's fees unless there is a recovery on the claim. You should not have to pay the attorney a retainer, nor do you pay him/her by the hour, the phone call, the letter, etc. But like any other contract, you should read the contract and UNDERSTAND all terms of the contract before you sign it!

Keep this in mind as well: the attorney works for you. If you do not feel he is giving your case the attention it needs, then I encourage you to schedule an appointment to meet with him. Make sure both of you are on the same page and time line about what will be happening on your case and when. There are several great lawyers out there handling workers' compensation and personal injury claims. Not all of them are great at interacting with their clients and keeping them informed about the work that is being done on their file. Err on the side of trying to work things out with your attorney and get your questions answered.

There may be a time when you do not have a good feeling about the attorney or his office staff that is handling your claim. If your efforts to communicate with him through calls and emails go unanswered, and you feel as though your problems are not resolved, it may be time to move on and get an opinion from another attorney. The fee agreement allows you to cancel the contract at any time - and you don't even have to explain your reason(s) to the attorney.

You will, however, possibly be responsible for paying the attorney for the reasonable value of the work performed or he may place a lien on the recovery in your case.

When the case settles, the attorney will also seek to be reimbursed for any costs advanced and expenses he incurred while working on your case. Every attorney charges for these costs and they are necessary to gather the material to present your claim to the insurance company or to prepare your case for trial. These expenses could include depositions, office meetings with doctors, narratives, or possibly other experts. At our law firm, we typically advance these costs for our client and pay the providers and experts for their services. We are willing to wait for a successful conclusion of the claim to get reimbursed. This way, our clients do not have to worry about coming out of pocket for these expenses - especially at a time where they are hurting - physically and financially.

The choice is certainly yours on whether or not you hire an attorney. Remember - you only have one shot at justice to recover all the cash and benefits to which you are entitled. I highly recommend you hire an attorney! Take advantage of the FREE consultation that some attorneys offer. This will allow you the opportunity to talk with the attorney to see if you have a good comfort level - with his knowledge of the law, as well as with his ability to interact with you in a genuine, caring, compassionate manner.

Chapter 15:
Conclusion

Chapter 15 - Conclusion

Three final things I want to stress to everyone that reads this book:

1.   This book is just a starting point for you to learn about your workers' compensation claim. Hopefully, it will provide you with the information you need so you can openly discuss the facts and the law as it applies to your claim with your attorney. Remember: No two cases are alike and this book is not and cannot be a "one size fits all" manual that applies to every workers' compensation claim in Georgia. Nothing can replace you taking the time to have the specific facts of your case thoroughly discussed with a lawyer that is experienced in handling workers' compensation claims.

2.   For the attorneys that practice workers' compensation law in Georgia - and do it the right way, I sincerely thank you and applaud you! Thank you for not using runners or for "chasing ambulances." Thank you for taking up the fight to be an advocate for the injured consumer. This battle is truly one between David and Goliath, but it is worth it. This book was written for you just as much as it was for the injured victims. Please read it and use it and give me your feedback. But please understand - no portion of the book can be copied or used in any way without my express, written permission. Should you have any questions, please do not hesitate to contact me.

3.   Please know that if you or a family member are injured on the job, you do not have to take on the battle with the insurance company and their lawyers by yourself. You owe it to your family - to yourself - to get the help you need. Our consultations are always free, completely confidential, and there is no obligation. You have nothing to lose by calling us, but think of all you can lose if you don't! The phone number is (770) 934-8000, or toll free 1 (888) 934-8100. You can also check out our website - www.GaryMartinHays.com. It is loaded with informative videos and articles regarding workers' compensation claims here in Georgia.

God Bless!

Gary Martin Hays

About The Author

About Gary Martin Hays:

Legal Accomplishments

Gary Martin Hays' legal accomplishments include being a member of the prestigious Multi-Million Dollar Advocates Forum, a society limited to those attorneys who have received a settlement or verdict of at least $2 million dollars. He has been recognized in Atlanta Magazine as one of Georgia's top workers' compensation lawyers as voted on by other lawyers in Georgia. Gary frequently lectures to other attorneys regarding personal injury and workers' compensation claims. He has been recognized as one of the Top 100 Trial Lawyers in Georgia since 2007 by the American Trial Lawyers' Association and recognized by Lawdragon as one of the leading Plaintiffs' Lawyers in America. He has also been recognized by the Georgia Trial Lawyers' Association for his community service efforts. His firm specializes in cases involving personal injury, wrongful death, workers' compensation, inadequate security, and social security disability claims. His videos on certain areas of Georgia Law have been watched over 5 Million times, making him the most viewed attorney in Georgia on Facebook and YouTube. Since 1993, his firm has helped over 40,000 injured victims and their families.

In The Media

Gary hosts "The Gary Martin Hays Show" on the CW Network, Atlanta's only daily legal television show. Gary is also the creator and host of "The Intersection: Where Country Meets The Cross," as featured on WKHX (KICKS 101.5 FM) in Atlanta. He also is the host of "The Wise Counsel Project" as featured on WFSH (FISH 104.7). Gary interviews men and women of faith, and asks them to share their "wise counsel" on how we can make better decisions in our daily lives. He has interviewed Bret Baier (Host of Special Report on Fox News), Comedian Jeff Foxworthy, Coach Tony Dungy, Actor Kirk Cameron, Governor Nathan Deal, and Dr. Alveda King.

He has been quoted in USA Today, The Wall Street Journal, and featured on over 250 online sites including Morningstar.com, CBS News's MoneyWatch.com, The Boston Globe, The New York Daily News, and The Miami Herald. Gary is also a 13 time best-selling author/co-author, including the #1 best-selling legal books, *The Authority On Personal Injury Claims in Georgia* and *The Authority On Workers' Compensation Claims in Georgia (this book!)*. Gary has been seen on countless television stations and shows, including Fox & Friends, CNN Headline News, ABC, CBS, NBC and Fox affiliates and has appeared on over 110 radio stations. He also served as an executive producer of a documentary entitled "Mi Casa Hogar" in

2013, which highlighted the amazing work done by this orphanage in Acapulco, Mexico. This project earned him his second Silver Telly Award, as his first was as an executive producer for "All Are Our Heroes" in 2010, a documentary regarding cancer survivors. A documentary about Gary and his law firm, "Stand & Serve", was featured on the Biography Channel in 2014, and this project also won a Silver Telly Award.

In The Community

Gary Martin Hays is not only a successful lawyer, but is a nationally recognized safety advocate who works tirelessly to educate our families and children on issues ranging from bullying to internet safety to abduction prevention. He currently serves on the Board of Directors of Operation Underground Railroad (O.U.R.), an organization that works to end human sex trafficking around the world. Over the last 10 years, Gary has pedaled an adult sized big wheel over 500 miles to raise money and awareness for various charities.

Civic Activities
- Founded Keep Georgia Safe in 2008, a non-profit whose mission is to provide safety education and crime prevention training in Georgia. This organization has trained over 80 state and local law enforcement officers on how to respond in the event a child is abducted.
- Gary is certified in Child Abduction Response techniques by Fox Valley Technical College and the FBI.

- His firm has given away over 1000 bicycle helmets to promote safety
- He has awarded 14 college scholarships to deserving students

Other Unique Endeavors

Gary has been a guest announcer on "Late Night with Jimmy Fallon." He has appeared in Nickelodeon's "See Dad Run" with Scott Baio, as well as in "Drop Dead Diva" on the A&E Network. He has performed on Broadway in "The Lion King," "Rock of Ages," and "Motown: The Musical." Gary has also interviewed and been interviewed by the great Larry King at his Woodland Hills, CA studio. Gary was featured in ex-CIA Operative Valerie Plame Wilson's novel "Burned" as a CIA weapons expert from Alabama. Bill Engvall played the White House Chief of Staff in "Sharknado 3" using his full name "Gary Martin Hays."